Vlogging

How to start a vlog and earn money with your vlog.

Vlogging tips and themes, cameras, videos, marketing, talent managers and sponsors.

by

Jordine Bowen

# Table of Contents

# Introduction

I want to thank you and congratulate you for purchasing this book which will help you understand the basics of vlogging and various ways to enhance your earnings from your vlog.

I am an aspiring vlogger and decided to dig into the world of vlogging, by investigating everything around it, before taking the plunch. I have interviewed vloggers, Internet marketers, sponsors and talent agencies. I have learned so much about vlogging that I decided to share this information with you.

Are you in awe of all those vlogging superstars? I know I am! Do you also dream to have a million subscribers one day? An aspiring vlogger is always caught up between the dreams that he has and the realities of the business. There are many vloggers that are doing great for themselves. You might feel overwhelmed when you look at their vlogs.

But, before you get all intimidated, you should remind yourself that even those successful vloggers had to start from somewhere. There was a time in their lives when they were in your position, when they were contemplating whether this is for them or not. This is how it begins. It is not going to be easy, but you will make it if you have the right passion and an ability to work hard.

The vloggers with over a million subscribers didn't get there in a day or a week or a month. It took them days and months together, and sometimes years to reach where they are. They started their vlogs with passion and a dedication. They worked hard and faced failures and success.

While they celebrated their success, they learnt from their failures. They kept moving and working hard, before they could gain any substantial profit from their vlogs. It takes time and you should be ready to invest that time.

Like any vlogger, it must be your dream to earn well through vlogging. This is very much possible, but you will have to give it your best. It is not enough for you to just generate high quality videos. But, in addition to this there are many other things that you will have to focus on. This book is an attempt to help you learn all this and more.

Vlog is a blog that has video as its content. YouTube provides a great platform for vloggers to broadcast their videos and earn money from them. YouTube made a debut in the year 2005. Since then, it is only growing. It was started with the idea of providing people a space to broadcast their work, views and opinions. This theme of YouTube has helped many budding vloggers to shape their careers.

There are vloggers who have made a fully-fledged business out of vlogging. Vlogging is slowly taking over the other entertainment sources. This is a great time for YouTube and the vloggers who broadcast their videos. The number of audience members is only increasing with time. This in turn provides a great opportunity for vloggers, who have become bigger celebrities than ever. They have followers, fans, book deals, brand deals and merchandise to their name.

It is important for you to understand that the business aspect of vlogging is a little complex and complicated. It is believed that the laws and rules are still taking shape. Vlogging is also evolving with the right set of rules with the growing vloggers and subscribers. If you are thinking of vlogging, you are also thinking about making money.

Nobody would work that hard for nothing. You can earn from various sources, such as brand deals, Google ad sense, book deals, music sales, tours and merchandise. If you tie up with a manager, they will help you earn more. For a part of your revenue, they will help you to earn through brand deals, ad sales and video production. As and when you become more and more popular as a vlogger, you will encounter more ways to earn money.

After reading this book, you will realize that all that you thought about vlogging was not entirely correct. You will learn many things that you never knew were critical to earning revenue from vlogs.

As you go further in the journey of being a vlogger, you will learn more and more ways to make better videos and earn better profit. But, even in the beginning, there are many things that you can do right. You should always remember that there are many vloggers out there and many of them are doing well.

You will have to establish yourself in a field that already has many great players. This is definitely not impossible. You should not feel daunted by the task that is ahead of you. You just need the right information to get started. This book will help you to get the information that you need.

**Note:** at the time of printing, all the websites listed or software mentioned in this book were working. As the Internet changes rapidly, some sites might no longer be live when you read this book or some software might no longer be available. That is, of course, out of our control.

By kind permission of Christine Clayfield, an Internet marketer, some information included in this book is written by Christine.
www.christineclayfield.com

# Chapter 1: Choosing the theme for your vlog

When vlogs first came about, they were used by the vloggers to document their entire day. These vloggers would take their audience through their day and will give them a sneak peak of their lives. But, with time this traditional definition of vlogging has changed. Now, people use a vlog for pretty much documenting anything.

As a vlogger, your vlog will give you a good platform to pursue your creative interests. If you are interested in teaching baking, you can create a vlog for that. If you have always wanted to be a chat show host, you can have your own vlog channel for the same. There are numerous creative interests that you can pursue via your vlog. You can also go the traditional route and use your vlog as a video diary to document your day for the audience.

To build the right vlog you will have to plan and balance many things. You should work on the length of the vlog, the pace of the video, your narration style and your mannerisms. No matter what you decide to vlog, your passion should come thorough to keep the audience engaged.

You will have to pay a lot of attention to the smallest of details. If you think that you lack in any of these attributes, you need not worry. If talking in a certain way does not come naturally to you, there is nothing to worry about.

A video blog or video log, abbreviated as a vlog, is a type of blog that creators share, generally on YouTube in video format. Vlogs also incorporate other video content taken from YouTube, pictures and other metadata.

Vlogs started out as people filming aspects of their lives and uploading them onto their personal blogs or YouTube channels, as a way for family and friends to catch up with them. But, at that time little did they know that these vlogs could earn them a fortune in the near future.

A vlogger can earn thorough endorsements with brands as well as earning money from the view count. Vlogging can also create endless opportunities that you never would have dreamed of, such as worldwide trips and working with multinational organisations.

In this book we will cover how to create your very own vlogging channel and how to grow your followers. The viewers want to watch someone engaging and unique, so this book aims to give you some top tips on vlogging. But, it is important that you understand that the book is not a guarantee to fame and money. The book will show you a way; the rest will depend on you. Above all, vlogging is a great way to document your life, like keeping a diary, so have some fun with it.

You can always acquire a talent and practice well to cultivate it. So, before you begin this journey, you should know that your hard work and your passion can help you overcome your shortcomings and get better at your vlogs with each passing day.

If you are beginning your journey of vlogging, you might be too keen and anxious. You would want to start earning right away. But, a little patience is required if you are looking for long term benefits. You should always look at the larger picture. To break it down for you to help you understand how you can earn money from your vlog, you should follow the given steps:

1.  First and foremost, you should choose a theme for your vlog. This is very important so you should spend enough time deciding this. To create a vlog, there needs to be a theme that you are comfortable with. You need to plan things in a long term way.

2.  You should work on a camera persona. This is important because you have to present yourself in a way that people like you. A vlog can only do well if there are subscribers and audience for it.

3.  Next step is to work on the content script. You should do your research well and should make sure that what you put out there is authentic and entertaining.

4.  The next step is shooting and the video. If you want to create a channel, you have to make good quality videos. Make sure you understand the basics of the equipment that you are using.

5.  After you have shot the video, you have to edit it. Everything that you shoot will not be interesting when you go back to it. There will be parts that you want to erase. Editing will help you to do so. You should also add effects that go well with your content.

6.  Once your video is uploaded, you have to do extensive marketing. People should know about your vlog and videos. This is only possible if you market the product well. Work towards getting subscribers and views.

7. Once you have reached a certain level in vlogging, you might need to contact a talent manager to improve your revenue. You can connect your blog and website to the vlog. You can collaborate with other vloggers. These are ways to increase your earnings.

## 1. A brief history

Vloggers are people like you and me. They are as normal as anyone of us. They have not acquired a master's degree in vlogging before doing what they do. They are individuals who film themselves conversing with the camera while doing different kinds of things. These videos are then uploaded on YouTube.

There are different kinds of vloggers and diverse sorts of vlogs. We will break the different types of vloggers down into categories later in this chapter. In general, vloggers are cheerful individuals who have something different to offer.

You might be following some of your idols on YouTube. But, do you ever wonder about the history of vlogging? How did it start? Who started it? Vlogging has come a long way since it started, as individuals and brands have realised its power to reach a mass audience.

Vlogging started in the year 2000, when Adam Kontras shot and posted a video of him alongside a blog section for his loved ones to see his cross country move from Ohio to L.A. It is said to be the first vlog. He posted his first video from an uninspiring inn in Springfield, Mo. The blog is still going, after 12 years, and is the longest-running video blog out there.

Throughout the next couple of years, a vast amount of vlogs began to appear around the Internet, however relatively few individuals were watching them. It was not until 2005 that vlogging exploded on the scene.

It was in that year that YouTube was created, meaning that the individuals making vlogs, as well as those watching them, expanded hugely. USA Today assessed in 2006 that 100 million videos were watched every day. Today, in 2017, this number is vastly growing.

In 2008, the vlog's effect could truly be felt amid the presidential election. Who can overlook Will.i.am's effective melody, "Yes We Can," woven throughout a discourse given by Barack Obama? The video became a standout amongst the most viewed political recordings ever. From that point forward, vlogging has been expanding in fame, due to the ease with which individuals can now shoot, transfer and share videos from their cell phone, iPad or tablet.

Vloggers utilize their virtual world for everything, from conventional journaling or short films and data sharing. With time, it has only become easier to document and vlog. Now, more and more people are joining this bandwagon.

Vlogging is the future, and we can either observe the change or grasp it ourselves. It is here to stay. This is something that you would understand as a budding vlogger.

## 2. The right vlog for you

It is very essential that you choose the right vlog for you. You should choose something that you are comfortable with and knowledgeable in. There is no use in starting a vlog and then realizing that you have very little knowledge about the topic. It is always better to do your research well.

When you are thinking hard about the kind of vlog to go ahead with, you should consider your true passion and the audience available in the niche. This will give you an idea as to how well you can do in the area.

If you fail to choose the right theme in the beginning, you only make it difficult for yourself in the later stages.

### Choose the topic that interests you.

It is very important that you choose a topic that truly interests you. There are many people who choose a topic just because it is a hot trend, but then fail to cope with the challenges of the subject. You should make sure that you don't make this mistake.

If you wish to do really well with your vlog, then you have to understand that you will have to do something that has not been done before. Why will someone want to watch your vlog if you tell them something that is already there? Even if you are doing something that has been done before, you have to do it in a unique way. A common mistake that many vloggers make is to copy someone else's style and content. If you do this, you will not go far.

You have to be really passionate about the subject that you wish to cover. For example, there are thousands of vlogs on makeup tutorials on the Internet and hundreds are joining in every day.

Just because everybody is doing it, you shouldn't jump on the bandwagon. If you have no real interest in makeup, your vlog will not do well. Make sure that you have some real knowledge in the subject that you choose to vlog on.

If you choose a topic that does not interest you, it will definitely show in your work. You will only be able to fake it once or twice, but slowly you will lose the passion and your work will suffer. You should know that the audience is very smart. They know when you fake it. You need to save yourself from falling into this trap.

The best way to zero down on the right subject for you is to do some research. Take a pen and paper and write down the various topics that you would want to make a vlog on. Now, go to the Internet and look for the various videos that are already available on these topics.

Understand what is already there and what new content you have to offer. Understand the shortcomings of those videos and list down how you can overcome these shortcomings in your videos. This preliminary research will help you to get acquainted with vlogging and will also help you to understand your skill set. You will also gain some confidence that is much needed when you venture into something like this.

**Consider the vlog as a serious commitment.**

You should know that a vlog is much more than fun. You might have a right over the content and you might have the flexibility of time, but that does not mean that this is a non-serious business. It is a serious and long term commitment.

The downside is that most often than not, you will not see immediate results. You will have to wait and still keep working at it. Are you willing to give in the time and efforts that it requires? Are you willing to be patient at times when you don't see results? Are you willing to improve your own knowledge about your chosen subject?

You should be prepared for what lies ahead of you. You should read various stories of different vloggers on how they had to struggle in the beginning. You need to be sure that you are ready for this journey that lies ahead of you.

**Choose your audience.**

A vlogger has to choose his audience. You should know what kind of people will enjoy your content. This is a two way road. When you choose a certain subject, you choose a certain kind of audience. And, if your work is good, then the audience also chooses you over the various other available options.

There are all kinds of people out there. There are many who love cooking, and there are many others who don't enjoy it. There are many who would love to watch comedy related videos, and there are many who will not enjoy them.

The basic point is that no matter what you choose to do, you will always have an audience. But, this audience will not waste their time on something that is not good. So, while you can be sure that you will find an audience for any subject that you choose, you should make efforts to engage your audience.

There is so much material on the Internet. The audience has too many choices. You have to make sure that you deserve the audience's attention and time.

You will in a way get a chance to choose your audience, but you have to engage them well. You should remember to be your first audience. Analyse your work as an audience would do.

**Combine skills or interest.**

When you do your research well, you will definitely find something that interests you enough to start a vlog on. But, if you fail at arriving at that one particular thing that interests you, then you can also consider the option to combine your various skills or interests.

This can turn out to be very useful for your new vlog. For example, if you like cracking jokes and also like cooking, you can look at creating a cookery show that allows you to be your humorous self. You combine the two talents and can come up with something that is unique and has not been done before.

It is always better to combine two skills if you are not sure of that one thing that can work in your favour. This will give you more confidence as a vlogger and will help you further improve and enhance your skills.

You can also think about teaming up with someone who has a particular skill that complements your skills. If you like your friend's way of talking and expressing himself, you can look at adding him and his skill as a part of your vlog. You can play along with various combinations as long as those combinations are good for your vlog.

The idea is that you can create a great vlog if you learn to play to your strengths. Even if there is something missing, you can cover up by being different and creative. Allow yourself to experiment creatively. Work on a few ideas before finalizing that one special idea.

**Evolve your style and keep looking.**

It is important that you understand that you are not required to stick to one style once you do it for your vlog. It is your vlog and you have the freedom to do whatever you want. You should always be prepared and ready to evolve your style. If you think that something is not working, then don't hesitate that to discard it. There should be no reason why you should attach yourself to it.

You should always look for better ways of presenting yourself and your content. You should keep an eye on what's working for you and what is not working. If you understand the journey of various successful vloggers, you will get to know that many of them took months and years to find their true voice and style.

And, til this happens, you need to keep looking. You will have to try many new things to understand about that one particular thing that your audience wants from you. Don't be afraid of experimenting new stuff.

Not everybody is good at everything. Even the most successful vloggers would have failed had they not chosen the right subject. It is important to find your true calling. This might take some time, but you will get there. To begin with, you should watch various kinds of vlogs on the Internet. This will give you an idea as what you can do.

Understand what other people are doing and how they are doing it. This will help you to understand what you can do well. It is extremely important to do your homework right. This will help you to make fewer mistakes in the future.

## 3. Who is your audience?

Once you know the subject of your vlog and your personal style that you would want to adopt, you should think about the kind of audience that you will cater to. People make vlogs and wish that more and more people should watch these vlogs.

Audience is a very important part of vlogging. It is something that you should think about in the very beginning of your journey. This will help you to avoid the pitfalls at a later stage.

To start with a vlog, you have to go with your instinct and the skill set that you already possess. You should have an idea of the kind of audience that will enjoy your vlogs. But, you should also know that this is just an idea. You can only learn as you go along on the journey.

There is no way to know everything definitely in the very beginning. You should trust your instincts and take some calculated risks. When you have an audience, you will also have different reactions. There will be people who will love your work, and there will also be people who will not find you interesting.

There might be many other people who will be ready to give you another chance. You should learn more about your audience as you go further. Understand what people are enjoying and what they are not enjoying.

Make note of things that you can bring on the table if you do similar kinds of vlogs. You should also look for the most popular vlogs to understand which kinds of videos attract maximum viewers. A point that should be noted here is that this can't be your only criteria when beginning a vlog.

You should look for subjects that attract maximum audience, but you should also have the ability to generate good videos on similar topics. You should also have something unique to offer to the audience.

It is very important to understand the content requirements of vlogs. While you might find certain videos on the Internet that you think you could have done better, you should also try to understand if there are reasons for omitting certain things from those videos.

Sometimes, the creator has to omit certain things to keep the length of the videos short. This is important because the creator of the videos should understand the optimum length of his videos. The audience will have a certain attention span for various topics. While a person might be able to watch a twenty minute cookery show, he might lose interest in a political show of such a length.

### 4. What should you vlog?

When you turn to vlogging, this is the first decision that you will have to take. What should you vlog? You might have already decided on what you want to do, but there is a chance that you are still confused.

It can be very overwhelming to choose a theme for your vlog. There are hundreds of things you can make a vlog about. Maybe you have many themes but are unable to decide as to which the best one is. If you browse the Internet, you will only get confused. Some tips that will help you to choose a theme for your vlog are as follows:

- You should understand that there is no perfect theme. What works the best for you might not work for the other person and vice versa.

- No matter how many themes you have in your head, you have to choose one. If you decide to make a random vlog with no consistent theme, you will not get anywhere. All the profitable vloggers use a particular theme for their vlogs. If you try to do too much, you will end up doing nothing.

- You should have a theme before you start. Don't make this mistake of uploading random videos and then deciding the theme.

- Do not follow anybody blindly. You can take ideas from the vlogs that you like, but blindly following someone is a big 'no'.

- You should write down all the themes that interest you. Write down the names of all the vlogs that you like. Now slowly go through all these vlogs. Make a list of things that you like and the things that you don't like. Make a list of all the areas that you think you could have done better. Also, write down why you think you could've been better. This study will help you a lot in your vlog.

Vloggers are individuals who film themselves conversing with the camera while doing a wide range of things and uploading this onto YouTube. There are distinctive sorts of vloggers and diverse sorts of vlogs. We will break the different types of vloggers down into categories.

Generally, vloggers are cheerful individuals who have something different to offer. However, it can be argued that the best vlogs are merely those showing vloggers messing around in their homes, with friends and family. Maybe because this makes them more relatable, and most people watch YouTube as a way to relax and switch off their brain.

A few of the different kinds of vlogs areas follows:

**A diary format**

Have you seen vlogs where the vlogger takes the viewers through his day? This is a vlog in dairy format. In this particular format, the presenter needs to take the viewers through his life. It is more or less like a diary in a video format. Remember the diaries or journals where you used to document your day as a child? The diary format allows the vlogger to document his day for the viewers.

These vloggers simply began discussing themselves and their lives to the camera in their rooms. Since they're charming and interesting, these vloggers are staggeringly popular. They create a diary of their lives by making a video every single day. AlfieDeyes of Pointlessblog, boyfriend of Zoella, is arguably the most famous daily vlogger on YouTube.

This is an interesting format because everybody likes to have a peep into other people's lives. It can be fun and interesting to see what other people do. The vlogger does not have to update a video every day. It is your choice as the vlogger as to when you want to shoot a video.

But, if you choose this format for your vlog, then it should be so interesting that people should wait to have a sneak peek into your life. There should be something in those videos that they find interesting and engaging. You should not bore your viewers by giving them a tour of a boring day. Nobody wants that.

You have to have, or at least you should pretend to have, a great and interesting life, if you wish to succeed in this format. There are a few vloggers who use the diary format in a little different manner. They just take the camera and speak to their viewers about random stuff. Not everybody can pull this off. You have to have some really good stuff that you can talk about every other day.

A simple way of making the diary format more engaging is to edit the videos well. You should edit out parts that you think are only adding monotony to the videos. Take your camera with you and shoot the major parts of your day. Talk to the viewers while you are shooting. After all this is done, do some good editing on the video. A good edit can really bring out the important and relevant parts of the video.

This format is definitely not for people who have a job where they can't take cameras. Even if you can, nobody would really be interested in watching you working at your desk. Either your job should be very interesting or you need to plan interesting stuff in your day to make this format profitable for you.

No matter what you are planning to do, it is important that you make sure that you are allowed to take the camera with you. Before you fix the plan, make all the necessary arrangements to be able to shoot your day.

You are the best judge of whether such videos are possible for you or not. If you have a daily routine where you go to places where cameras are not allowed, then this can be difficult for you. There are many people who find this format cumbersome. You need to be sure that you like the diary format and it excites you. If you are excited then it will be easier for you to go on even when there are hurdles on the way.

There are many popular vloggers on the Internet that swear by this format. People love watching their videos to know what these vloggers are up to. You can also add some funny banter as you are recording the videos to make the videos fun and entertaining. You can also add some surprise elements for the viewer so that the viewer looks forward to your updates and videos.

There can be some variations to this format. You can make a diet only vlog, where you make videos on what you ate during the day. You can also show recipes of a few dishes in these videos. There are no rules as such, so you can make your own variations.

As long as people on the Internet find your videos fun and watch them, you are good. The idea is to capture the interest of the viewer. You can come up with many ways to do so. If you are successful, there is nothing like that. Even if you are not successful in the beginning, you still have many ways and chances to improve and try something new.

**Entertainment vlogs**

There are many other vlogs that have come into existence in the past few years.

Vloggers are discovering new and innovative ways to make their videos. They are coming up with new ideas for the content of the videos. You can also try new and innovative things if you wish to. But, if you are too confused and unsure, then it is better to stick to the formats that already exist and are popular. This minimises your chances to make errors.

There are many kinds of entertainment vlogs. There is no definitive list of entertainment vlogs from which you can just pick one. But, to have an idea of what entertainment vlogs are all about, a small list is being provided:

- Street prank videos or any other pranks
- Videos where you throw and accept challenges
- Gaming videos
- Singing and dancing videos
- Instrument playing

In a singing and dancing video, you could sing or dance or do both. There are so many such videos on the Internet. You have to be exceptional in your talent if you want to do well in this format. It is an entertainment vlog, so the audience needs to be entertained.

You will have to find new and innovative ways to be different from what people in the same format are doing. It is never wrong to do something that someone else is doing, but you have to be better in some respect. If you are also providing the exact same content as the other people, why should anybody come to your vlog?

In street prank videos, you can play pranks with people on the road. This can be fun for people to watch. You will encounter all kinds of people on the streets. Some will take your prank in a good spirit and some won't. Even if they are not very supportive you can shoot it and put it in your video. The viewers will have fun watching the real life reactions.

You can also ask questions to people on the streets, if you don't want to do any pranks. Take a fun question that will guarantee all kinds of reactions. Now, take the camera and go to the streets. Ask the people to answer your question. Record their answers. You are going to surprised yourself. This can be some good content for your viewers.

If you can come up with entertaining questions and can keep the whole thing fun with some humour then you can expect many people to watch your videos. People want a break and want to have some fun. So, make sure you give them something worth watching.

**Gaming vlogs**

Another popular genre is the gaming videos. There are many entertaining and popular games. You can play these games and shoot the entire process. Give instructions to the viewer when you are playing as to what you are doing and what is happening. This can be entertaining and can also be fun for people who are looking for some instructions on certain online games.

Gaming vloggers are vloggers who commentate on a game they are playing. Their principal ability is their capacity to think of fresh and novel methods for swearing at zombies! These vloggers are fiercely prevalent with young men (and a few young ladies) of all ages. Internationally the most well-known of these is PewDiePie (Felix Arvid Ulf Kjellberg) a Sweden-born, Brighton based 24 year old. He is as of now the world's most well-known vloggers, and he has the most subscribers on YouTube! A lot of these gaming vloggers every so often make different sorts of vlogs, for example, diary vlogs or prank vlogs, but they are mainly known for their gaming content.

Now, the catch here is that there are so many gaming vlogs already on YouTube. If you go for a game that is not very popular, then not many people will watch your videos. You have to have the passion for the game and there should be the right audience for the same.

On the other hand, if you go for a game that is highly popular then there will be hundreds of vlogs on the same. So, you have to find a way where you can vlog a game that will be watched. It goes without saying that for these videos, you should have an interest in gaming. A person who is not genuinely interested in gaming will only mess this format up.

## Educational vlogs

Another format that is very profitable is the making of educational vlogs. There are many kinds of educational vlogs. The main aim of these vlogs is to impart some kind of knowledge to the viewers. They teach the viewer something new. More and more vloggers are experimenting with this kind of vlogging. In fact, new styles and genres are being implemented every day.

Though they are educational, they need to be made entertaining. You have to find a way to be funny and still impart the desired knowledge to the audience. It can be a little challenging, but if you are fully aware of what you are doing and what you want to do, it will get better.

There are many kinds of educational vlogs that can be made. Some of them are as follows:

- How to videos
- Fashion tutorials
- Make up tutorials
- Exercise tutorials
- Weight loss videos
- Electronic gadgets related vlog
- Diet related videos
- Travel
- Simple tricks in various subjects
- Talking about a specific subject, such as Physics
- Imparting knowledge on anything you are experienced in

If you are good at something, you can start a vlog and share your knowledge with the world. You should have enough passion and knowledge on the topic that you choose if you wish to do well in this format. For example, if you choose make up tutorials, then you need to be really talented. If you know nothing about make up, then how will you teach others? You have to have the right knowledge.

It is better to choose a topic that falls under your comfort zone. There is no point in trying something that you can't excel in. You have to make several videos on the topic, so it is only important that you know the topic well.

In addition, you have to look for ways to make your vlog better than the others. There are so many make up tutorials on the internet. Why should anyone watch your videos? What special will you offer? Maybe you can concentrate on things that others have missed.

You need to do your research well if you wish to gain profits from your vlogs in the long run. Just like the makeup tutorials, you can have tutorials on anything and everything. How to videos are very popular on the internet.

One of the most popular and prevalent vloggers are the beauty vloggers. These vlogs talk about fashion, beauty, plus hair and makeup guidance. This can incorporate the 'haul' video where the vlogger goes shopping, more often than not for clothes & makeup, and demonstrates to us what they have purchased.

Zoella is arguably the biggest beauty vlogger on YouTube; with over 14million subscribers, but smaller fashion vloggers are also increasing in popularity, such as Inthefrow. These vloggers are typically women however male makeup artist gossmakeupartist is a standout amongst the most well-known beauty vloggers.

There are also educational vloggers, such as Diana Cowan, who makes physics interesting to kids all over the world! This is an example of how YouTube and vlogging can transport you to fame, but not in the Hollywood sense. These vlogs can teach their viewers about anything, but the fact that this platform enables learning is astounding.

Travel vloggers are also very popular on YouTube, as they allow you to visit places all over the world, just by sitting behind your computer screen at home in your pyjamas. Funforlouis is a very popular travel vlogger. He travels all over the world and films it and uploads it onto YouTube. It is becoming a more utilised way of planning trips than buying travel guides or going to the travel agent, as the vlogs are from a real persons perspective.

Many of the above discussed vloggers have the opportunity to travel through their vlogging career, to events or meeting fans, but it is not their primary content, as it is for travel vloggers. Travel vloggers will document their travels and will share it with the viewers. As a viewer, it is great to see exotic places on YouTube, when you know you personally can't see every place on earth.

With the current worldwide trend of veganism, or just healthy eating becoming increasingly popular, there are also food vloggers or dieticians who create vlogs to spread this trend further. They create recipes or show you 'what they eat in a day', in order to inspire viewers to adopt this new healthy lifestyle.

Jessbeautician is an example of a foodvlogger, as well as Niomi Smart. Or, there are food vloggers that are the total opposite, such as Furiospete, who does crazy food challenges involving eating as much as he can in a short amount of time, or having 10,000 calories in one day.

# Chapter 2: Developing a camera persona

There is a certain persona that you would have to maintain in front of the camera. If you follow certain vlogs, you will notice that all these vloggers have a specific way of speaking and behaving in front of the camera. Now, this persona that they maintain in front of the camera can be totally opposite to how they behave in normal life.

You will also have to develop a persona that is pleasing in front of the camera. This is important to keep the audience engaged. Over time, this can also become your signature style and can add to your success and popularity. Like the many other vloggers, you will have to work on developing a voice that you will use for your vlog.

Along with the voice modulations, you will also have to work on developing certain mannerisms that are pleasant in front of the camera. This is a very important aspect that a new vlogger needs to understand. You might take some time to understand this and then develop a style, but you will get there as long as you are trying.

The way you speak with your family and friends in real life and the way you would speak in front of the camera will be different. Even if you have to speak in front of thousands of people in real life, you might not need to modulate the way you speak.

You can speak normally by letting the words flow naturally one after the other at a normal pace. This will be enough for the live audience to follow you. But, if you want your television or vlog audience to follow you clearly, there are a few modulations that you can't do without.

When you speak in front of the camera, you need to do certain modulations. If you closely follow anchors on television, you will notice the modulations they make to their voices in front of the camera. These anchors and hosts need to enunciate the words to sound perfect to the audience that watches them and listens to them in front of the television set.

For the camera, you would have to speak by laying more emphasis on the words that you utter. You will have to give special emphasis on the enunciation of the words. It is like speaking in a more animated way, which you will never do in your real life.

But, you can't do without it in front of the camera. You will have to bring in certain variations in your tone when you express yourself. This is something that you will learn by observing others who do the same and also by practicing well.

It becomes very important to work on a camera personality for a vlog. This is something that you can skip when you are into blogging. You are not in front of the people when you are blogging, so you can easily skip this part. The next section will help you to understand the difference between a blog and vlog.

**1.Blogging versus Vlogging**

Blogging on camera is often termed as vlogging. While blogging, a person has the freedom to express his opinions and views in a journal format on a website, vlogging allows the same in a video format. A vlog allows more freedom of creativity to the vlogger.

The vlogger can use different antics to impress the audiences. It is easier to create a bond with the viewers. While there are great opportunities to form a direct connect with the viewers, there is also a chance of things going terribly wrong.

A lot more hard work is required in creating a vlog. You need content and a style of presenting the same in a blog. You need to present the same along with yourself in a vlog. The viewers will judge you in terms of the location you choose, your camera personality and your entertainment level. You need to focus on yourself as much as you would focus on the content.

When it comes from making good revenue, both blogging and vlogging are extremely powerful tools for brands. Be it novice blog owners, beauty gurus on YouTube, or experienced experts in the field of social media marketing, everybody is attempting to enhance their businesses using vlogging and also blogging.

For very few vloggers, vlogging is their only method of income. To begin, with, they have a linked website or blog to increase their revenue. Apart for this, there are brand deals and advertisements.

Both blogging and vlogging are very powerful, so it is essential to know which strategy for communication is ideal for you and your business. Should you have a vlog or blog or both?

**Advantages of Blogging**

Blogging, in the least complex terms, resembles an online 'log', where the author can share their thoughts, feelings, or anything they want. Publishing blogs have turned into a standard way for entrepreneurs and companies to advertise, as they offer an extraordinary platform to connect with potential consumers.

You might have seen many blogs on the Internet. You too can create one. You can use your blog only for business related purposes or can create a personal blog, where you share your thoughts and opinions with the readers of the blog.

The blogs are not difficult to set up and don't require any capital input. You can easily create a blog with no investment. All you need to do is focus on the content. Blogger, WordPress, Tumblr or Pen.io, can be set-up without spending a penny. Blogging also does not require any software to download or programmes to install.

The main things you may require are a tablet or a laptop, along with a working Internet connection. By utilizing strategies like affiliate marketing, or via optimizing your blogs utilizing legitimate SEO, you can earn a living by posting blog posts online.

Further, blogs have been around for much longer than vlogs have, and blogs have stood the test of time as a money-maker for the creator. On the other hand, it is said that vlogging can make you more money.

Before explaining the disadvantages of blogging, let me explain what SEO is as I've just mentioned SEO.

SEO stands for Search Engine Optimization or how to be shown with your videos in Google or on video sites, when somebody searches for your name/videos.

SEO is important whatever kind of vlogger you want to be. Therefore a word about SEO. It is not the aim of this book to go into too much details about SEO but a few important words are needed here as it is vitally important that you do use SEO in your vlogs.

SEO is the process of developing your website with a view to rank in Google in the organic or natural listings (not paid listings) following certain rules, which are mostly keyword (a keyword is whatever someone types in the search engine or search bar) related. SEO is a technique which, when applied correctly, can result in the search engines finding your site/videos and ranking it higher than millions of other sites/videos. SEO can be used in the 'about' section of your YouTube channel, as well as in the description of your videos and the title.

SEO is something that any new online business must familiarize themselves with. After all, when it's done correctly, it is your ticket to true online success.

While you don't have to be a complete expert at SEO to start building your website business, it will be extremely helpful if you are somewhat familiar with SEO and what it can do for you. Therefore, I strongly recommend at least reading the Beginner's Guide to SEO on www.moz.com before delving too deep into launching your vlog. You'll be amazed at how much it can help you build your site, research competition and market your site later on. You can download the guide here: https://moz.com/beginners-guide-to-seo

The most important thing to remember: when you upload your video(s), give them a title with your keyword e.g. DON'T call your video "beautytips" but instead call your video"YourNameHereBeautyTips".

There are books just about SEO therefore it is impossible to including everything you need to know in this book.

For great SEO information and any other Internet terminology and how to earn money online (outside vlogging), I recommend the book "From Newbie to Millionaire" by Christine Clayfield (www.christineclayfield.com ), which you can buy on Amazon.

## The Disadvantages of Blogging

While there are many advantages of blogging, there are a few disadvantages also. Before you decide that this is the thing for you, you should also understand the disadvantages well.

If you want to start a blog to make a living out of it, it is essential that you learn about SEO. Finding out about keywords, meta tagging, and including a fitting description is important to guarantee that your blog appears in the first few pages on search engines such as Google.

Along with having great SEO knowledge, you should keep your blog updated on a constant & regular basis. Once your readers begin to appreciate reading your blog, they will want to come back to your blog and read more, which means you always have to be on top of things and constantly update it.

If your blog entries are too spaced out, leaving too much time between each post, readers may begin to lose enthusiasm for reading. This also goes hand-in-hand with the ability to write great content and take appealing pictures for the blog post, in order to attract people to your page. This is timely work and taking great photos can require extra lighting and special lenses to carry around to locations.

## The Advantage of Vlogging

Setting up a decent vlog is not exceptionally difficult on the off chance that you have the correct sort of gear. Numerous vloggers set up YouTube accounts which are completely free and easy to use. Vlogging does not require you to have excellent written or even oral communication, as vlogging is more geared toward having a casual conversation with the viewer.

Vlogs also have more potential to go viral than blogs do. Videos are now shared all over the internet. Everybody has a video to share. If you scroll through your face book for example, you will see videos all over your feed. This is how powerful this medium has become. If money and fame are what you are after, vlogging may be your best bet.

Pople can relate more to a video than text. It is easier to watch a video than to read text. There might be many people who would enjoy blogs more than vlogs, but in general videos are the trend today. And, they will remain for the years to come.

### The Disadvantage of Vlogging

One disadvantage of vlogging is that you have to be on camera, rather than being anonymous behind your computer screen, as you are with blogging. This is the thing that many people find extremely uncomfortable.

If you are shy or insecure, blogging is definitely preferred over vlogging, but this can mean that the people vlogging on YouTube are all extroverted. This is where you can come in if you are shy, and that can be your niche. Also, you probably will need high quality camera equipment and lights in order to create the most visually appealing vlog.

You will also need to buy some editing software for your computer, such as final cut, which vloggers use to edit their vlog footage, adding background music for example. All of these costs do add up, and seeing as vlogging is not a guaranteed job or money maker, this can be something that puts people off starting to vlog.

Another disadvantage of vlogging over blogging is that a vlog is not as easily edited one it is published. For example, on a blog post, the host can quickly log in and change the content without having to publish a new blog post. But with a vlog, the vlog must be taken down and re-uploaded if any edits are to be made.

Vlogs are additionally very time-consuming to create. It can take anywhere in the range of 2 to 4 hours to record, edit and also publish a vlog. It can also take longer than that depending on the content of your vlog. You have to devote some quality time to your vlog if you are looking for some good returns in the near future.

### Vlogging versus Blogging

The decision lies altogether with the individual who is either beginning a blog or a vlog. Both blogging and vlogging have their advantages and disadvantages, so these need to be investigated before your make your choice.

On the off chance that you are not an extraordinary author, and think that it's simpler to address individuals personally, vlogs may be your best bet. However, if you are very shy and find it difficult to communicate through writing, blogging may be your preferred method of sharing.

Obviously, you could run a vlog parallel to a blog. This makes it simpler to draw in more readers & viewers and to get their thoughts through different modes of interaction.

## 2.Analyse your personality off camera

To develop a persona in front of the camera, it is extremely important that you access your personality off camera. This will help you to know how much work you need to do on yourself. Do your friends and family describe you as boring or entertaining? Do you think you are a fun person in normal life?

This assessment is done to know what needs to be done to develop a good camera persona. So, remember to be true to yourself. Even if people around you term you as non-entertaining and boring, it is absolutely fine. You will just need to work a little harder on yourself to develop a pleasing style of speaking and behaving in front of the camera.

Your videos will be watched not just for the content that they have to offer, but also for your own personal style. Nobody would want to watch a video where the presenter looks bored and tired, even if you have the best content to offer. It is a right mix of everything that helps in making great videos.

Your camera personality is as important as the content of the video. So, it is only important that you spend a good amount of time in analysing your real personality and then developing a pleasing one for the camera and for all those people who would watch you in your videos.

## Don't get disheartened

It is extremely important that you don't get disheartened. Even if you feel that you lack energy in comparison to other vloggers, you can still do it. You might be surprised to know that many successful media persons and vloggers have a very boring and non-entertaining personality off the camera.

They have worked to build an entertaining personality for the audience and the camera. If they can do it, so can you. So, it is important that you accept the challenge and don't get disheartened.

The point is to be prepared before you venture into the world of vlogs. There is no point making boring vlogs and then getting rejected by the audience. You will only get more disheartened.

It is better to work on your camera personality before you publish your vlogs. You should understand that if you work on yourself and learn the basic tools of editing videos, you can also make interesting and fun videos like other vloggers.

If you spend some time watching popular videos, you will see that the presenter is always full of energy. The person talks and behaves in a very energetic way. You need to have this form of energy in front of the camera if you wish to keep your video gripping.

A pleasing personality will in a way force you to come back for more. Haven't you gone back to certain videos just because the person was very pleasing? This happens all the time and with everybody.

Your energy should be gripping and contagious. The viewer should feel infected by the energy. If you are very reserved and low in energy in real life, then you need to work on your personality in front of the camera.

On the other hand, if you are a very energetic person, then you should know that this energy should be the minimum amount of energy that is required to be translated well in front of the camera. You can't go low on energy just because you are feeling low.

### 3. Choose a good time to shoot videos

You should always choose a good time to shoot videos. There is no need to get up at 5 am and shoot a video. On the other hand, if you feel extremely upbeat and energetic at that part of the day, then you should definitely choose to do it at 5 am. The point is to know the right time for you.

Different people feel upbeat at different times. Spend some time and energy to understand your cycle. This is important so that you can use it to your advantage. Do you feel lethargic in the evening? Do you feel energetic an upbeat after your morning meal? Make a note of all your moods at different parts of the day.

Compare and analyse various days. This will definitely help you understand your moods better. You should try to schedule your video shoots at times when you are full of energy. At times, this might not be possible. But, you should try to do it as much as possible. If you are thinking that you will have to spend a large amount of money to get good lighting, then you are wrong.

As you progress as a vlogger, you can look to buy high end equipment for good lighting for your vlog. You will find many lighting sources that will add to the quality of your videos. But, at this stage, this is completely redundant. You don't need to buy any such equipment. You can do well with whatever light sources you have in your home.

A simple way of making the best videos with a minimum investment is to shoot these videos in broad daylight. This is the simplest way to get good quality videos.

Sun could be your natural light source and the quality of the videos will be great. This could be constraint for many, but if you can do it, then it would be great. You will have to plan your day in a way that you can shoot in the mornings. You should be ready with the content beforehand.

If you are unable to shoot during day times, then you can also shoot good videos in your house in the most cost effective way. If you switch on all the bulbs and tube lights in your room, you will be able to shoot good videos.

If you feel that these light sources are not enough, then you can look at buying some table lamps as an option. This will not cost you much, but will help you to get the desired effect. When you shoot the video, you just need to face all the table lamps that you are using towards your direction. If you like the idea of buying desk lamp, then you need to make sure that the lamp has an adjustable head. If it is not adjustable, you will not be able to point in the direction that you wish to point to.

You should use white light bulbs and not yellow light bulbs to get a good lighting effect. These simple ways will help you get good quality light without having to invest much.

### 4. Practice in front of the camera

A simple way to work on your energy levels is to practice in front of the camera. You don't have to be prepared with a script. Just turn on the camera and pretend that you are speaking for your vlog. While you jabber away in front of the camera, you will slowly understand which words need more emphasis than the others. You will understand that you can't speak in one tone. You have to modulate.

As an experiment, speak normally in front of the camera. When you are done, go back to your video and watch yourself. You will see for yourself that you sound and look boring when you speak without any modulations. This will help you to understand the difference between speaking normally and speaking in front of the camera.

You should record multiple videos where you should try different modulations. You should also practice enunciation and laying emphasis on various words. Also, be more energetic in your body movement. Understand the frame and the range of the camera. In the given range, you should try moving about while talking.

As a budding vlogger, you basically need to try everything out so that you know what works for you. You should also make sure that at no point, you look like you are faking your energy levels. Feel good and energetic and bring that energy from within. What you pretend will be clearly caught on the camera. So, it is always better to be as real as possible.

**Understanding the camera angles**

While you practice in front of the camera, you should also get used to the space that the camera allows you. You shouldn't be out of focus for the camera. This will take some time and practice from your side. Every time you make a practice video, check whether you went out of the scope at any time during the video.

Make sure that you don't repeat the same mistakes in the next video. The idea is to be energetic and involve lots of movements while making the videos, and also do all this in the scope of the camera.

The reason behind being so particular about the camera location is that once you get used to the frame and the scope, you will get time to work on your persona. If every time you switch on the camera, you have to worry about whether the camera is capturing you or not, then how will you focus on the other important aspects.

You need to be done with these basic things in the beginning so that you can focus on your talking style and presenting style in front of the camera.

Another point that needs to be kept in mind is that you shouldn't get very near to the camera. You need to maintain a good distance from the same. In technical terms, you need to maintain a medium close up. A medium close up is when you are at a distance from a camera such that your upper body is clearly visible. This is considered to be just right for vlogs.

Of course you can change and modulate as you go along while making your vlogs. But, in the beginning keep this as a simple rule for yourself.

You might have chosen a background for yourself. You should also not get very near to your background. You have to be at the right place for the camera to capture you well. You will slowly understand your camera and its limitations. You will also learn to adjust according to that. But, make an effort to understand various camera angles for your videos.

## Exaggerate

After you have understood the camera angles, you will understand the frame in front of the camera better. You will know how much space you have to freely move around. Once you are done understanding this, you need to work on your movements and speaking style.

Just switch on the camera and move about in front of the camera. Speak anything, but be more animated than your usual self. Make use of your hand movements when you are stressing a point. Open your mouth more than usual. In short, just exaggerate everything a bit. This might feel a little odd to you in the beginning, but you will realize that this will look fine in front of the camera.

If you like what you have done, then change your style in the next practice video. This is a simple exercise to build a strong camera persona. You should not hesitate in learning from vloggers whose style you admire. Try to understand how they do it. This will help you in your own journey.

The mantra is to keep trying. You will finally find a style and voice that suits you and helps you in your vlog journey. Once you are a little comfortable with the camera, you should aim at speaking for longer durations. Even if you intend to make short videos, practice for longer durations. This will give you enough time to get used to a style. You can record these videos and see for yourself whether you need to tweak something or not.

You don't need a script to prepare these practice videos. Just start the camera and speak anything for at least 4-5 minutes with lots of energy and movements. But, if you find it difficult to talk for so long without a script, then you can go ahead and take a newspaper article for practice or write some script on your own.

## 5. Understand what the viewer is looking for

You have to make an attempt to understand what the viewers are looking for. This is easier said than done. But, think about this problem as an audience first and then as a vlogger. Would you want to watch someone who looks very morose? Would you want to waste your time on someone who is very dull and lethargic? Would you want to watch a video in which the presenter looks like he is extremely bored? When you answer these questions as an audience and a viewer of videos, you will get your answers.

Keep these points in mind while you are working on your personality for the camera. Make sure that your talking style does not bore the viewer. You have to make sure that the viewer should love and not repel your personality as a presenter.

This might not seem like a very important point to a newbie, but if you don't figure out these things in the beginning, you might find it difficult to control them at a later stage.

The more you understand the relevance of a viewer's impact on a vlog, the better you'll do for yourself. You have to impress the people out there. It is not possible to impress them all, but you have to impress the section of people that like your kind of work and who follow your work. You have to know what they expect from you.

People have so much going on in their routine lives. Your future audience will also have a lot going on. They will personally know many boring and lethargic people. While they might find it difficult to get rid of these people in real life, it is very simple for them to get rid of a boring vlogger.

They are not under any obligation to watch your videos. You have to remember this simple point at all times. They will only watch you if you offer them something in terms of content and your style. People have no patience and time. They might not give you another chance. So, you have to put your best foot forward.

Think from the audience's point of view when you plan anything for your vlog. This will help you to work harder on the things that work and discard the stuff that does not work. While it is important to keep the things that work, it is all the more critical to know the things that are not working in your favour. You have to rid of anything that is not contributing towards your success as a vlogger.

# Chapter 3: Preparing the content script

Vlog is an abbreviated variant of the word video blog or video log. A vlog is basically a blog that incorporates or comprises of video footage, which can include supporting text and images.

It is your average person filming their lives and uploading it for their viewers to see on YouTube. This can be of every-day activities such as watching TV and walking the dog, or more extravagant things such as traveling and skydiving.

No matter how much you work on the other aspects of your vlog, everything can go to waste in absence of a good script. There is no vlogger who can deny the importance of a content script in his vlogs. If you wish to succeed as a vlogger, you should make it a point to work on your content right from the beginning.

Your script should be crisp and engaging. It should invite the viewer and should also have him hooked. Nobody has the time to waste on badly presented content.

This chapter will help you understand how you can prepare a good content script. It should be noted here that the kind of vlog you are looking to create will determine the kind of script that you should be writing. For example, if you are going the traditional way in which you take the viewer through your day, your script will be very different from other vlogging styles.

There are many formats where you will be using impromptu speech. But, no matter what kind of vlog you are looking to create, preparation of the content is a given. You should know what you will present and how you will present it.

When you work on the content, your biggest challenge will be to present all the relevant information in a given time. After all, you would want to keep the videos concise and to the point. You would slowly get there. All you need is the right amount of preparation and practice.

## 1. Importance of a content script

If you are still debating in your head whether you need a script ot not, then this section will help to clear your doubts. Preparing a good script and rehearsing it well only shows your dedication towards your craft. This, in any way, does not mean that you are taking an easier route. It only means that you believe in preparing well, and there is nothing wrong in that.

There are a few vloggers who believe that preparing a script hampers with their natural flow. They feel constricted and bound. They believe that this affects their performance in the videos. These vloggers believe in keeping it natural. They will just switch on the camera and speak about the topic that they had intended to speak on. This style is known as the extempore style.

You also have the option to choose this style if you feel that you are at your best when you have no script and rules that bind you. A very important point that needs to be noted here is that the vloggers that use this style for communicating with the viewers are very few in numbers. You should also note that these vloggers are very good at what they do and have taken years to reach here. You need to study their history before you blindly follow them.

Another important point that you should note here is that most top vloggers use the simple style of preparing a script and rehearsing it well. They know that when you are well prepared, it takes off the entire load from you when you are filming these videos. They know that a good content script is like winning the half battle.

You can be sure that if you are able to present the content in a good way, your job as the vlogger is done. It is always better to take this route and work on your content well in advance. You can even practice with both the methods and see for yourself which suits you better.

While you are contemplating and deciding which style works for you the best, you should consider the following points:

- Vlogging is different from television: Vlogging is very different from television. There are no overhead costs that an agency will have to suffer if you don't deliver on time. It is important that you meet your personal deadlines, but it is also important that you understand your own style well. You can take your time and experiment. There is no fixed time slot when your programme goes on air. You have the liberty to decide for yourself. It is very important that you make use of this opportunity that is given to you.

- You are not live: You should understand that you are not live. Your viewers are not watching you at the same time when you are shooting the videos. You have the choice to shoot, re-shoot or even cancel the entire video. You have all the time to decide how you want the things to be done. It is important that you understand this that all the successful vloggers take time with their script. They shoot, re-work on the script as per needed and then shoot again. You can relax and work on your content because you are your own boss.

- Preparation is the key: You should remember that when you are not prepared, it will show on the camera. The camera will capture your fumbles and lack of preparation and the viewers will perceive this as a lack of interest and will.

If you adopt the extempore style, you can add a lot of natural realism to your videos. But, this is a very difficult style. You can completely lose it midway. It is better to prepare a good content and present in the most realistic way as possible. Until and unless you are hundred per cent sure that the extempore is your style, you should go for preparation of script. Even if you have one per cent of a doubt, it is better to do the route that has lesser chances of errors.

It should also be noted here that even if you want to adopt the extempore style to present your videos, you have to be prepared in a certain way. You might not sit and prepare the content script, but you will still have to be updated about the topic. You can't talk about something that you don't know about.

You will have to prepare well and make sure that your knowledge is up to date. People will not come back to your videos if they are not learning something from you. You should make sure that your content, whether it is rehearsed or not, is thorough and has something to offer to everyone. This is the only reason people would want to come back to your videos again and again. So, the point is that you can choose to prepare a content script or not, but whatever you choose, you will still have to be well prepared.

## 2. Why do you need a script for a traditional vlog?

If you are going for a traditional vlog, then you might be wondering as to why you need to be prepared with a content script. Traditionally, vlogs were used to film the entire day of the vlogger. The vlogger would film a day in his life and take the viewers through his daily activities.

You might think that something like filming a day in one's life might not require any preparation at all. You might believe that it will all happen spontaneously. This is not true. If you are a budding vlogger, then it is important for you to know that you will have to put in some amount of efforts and preparation even to look spontaneous.

If you are filming your days, you will have to plan and prepare certain activities to keep the viewer interested. If your Sunday is exactly like your Saturday and Monday, then why would the viewer want to come back to the vlog? You will have to plan activities.

You can also use the opportunity given to you by talking about things that are close to you. You can use the vlog to speak about your personal life and issues.

You can also use this platform to talk about bigger issues. It can get very monotonous for the viewer if you don't make an effort to introduce variations at various stages. This is exactly where the content scrip will help you. You can work on an interesting script for your viewers even when you are taking them through your day.

Vlogging is a great way to put forth your opinions. There is so much happening in the world. You might have a lot to say, but no one to listen. You can use the opportunity of your vlog to voice your opinions. This will give you an outlet and will give your viewers or audience an insight into your mind and life. But, it is important that this opinion sharing shouldn't become a rant.

You have to take efforts to make things presentable. This is exactly where a content script will help you. A concise and precise content script will help you to voice your opinions and also influence the viewer in the right way.

### 3.Three main styles of presenting the videos

Different vloggers choose different styles to present their videos. They go by their instincts and their experience. After making many videos and practicing for hours, they know what works for them and what does not. You should also choose something that works well for you and your vlog.

While you are deciding how you would want to present your videos, this section will help you a lot. The three main styles to present a vlog are as follows:

**No script at all:** This is a style in which the presenter will not be preparing a formal script for the vlog. There are no rehearsed lines. It is more like an extempore where the vlogger starts the camera and speaks without a script. This style is followed by vloggers who know that they perform better without a script. It is not for people who fumble for words each time they are supposed to speak.

It should be clearly noted here that this style of presenting the videos promotes a no script at all style, but it does not mean that no preparation goes into it. Even with no script, there has to be enough preparation. You can't cook without the raw materials. It is as simple as that.

You can't just start the camera and blabber. Even without the script, you have to know what you will be speaking about and how long you would be speaking. It is important to have an idea about the same.

A lot of research and preparation goes in this style of presenting the videos. The vlogger should select a subject and research exhaustively on the topic. It is important that when the vlogger decides to shoot the video, he has a lot of knowledge about the subject, no matter what the subject is.

It is also important to be in tune with the latest developments in the subject. The knowledge that you had one year back on the subject might or might not be relevant. It is very important to be updated.

If you choose this style of presentation in your vlog, then remember to be well informed. It is important to have a back-up of knowledge in this kind of presentation.

You need to understand different perspectives of the same topic. The viewer is interested in your point of view that is why he is watching your video. You should not just blabber dictionary definitions. It is highly important that you have your own point of view on the subject that you share in the video.

In this style, you will have no script to consult while shooting your videos, but you will have to make a lot of mental notes. You will have to rely on these mental notes when you are making the videos. When you are researching for the subject, make sure that you understand the subject well and make a lot of mental notes. These notes will help you when you are in front of the camera.

This style of presenting the videos is liked because of the spontaneity that the videos bring. The presenter has no script. It is more like talking intuitively on what he really thinks and feels. It is more real, but this style should only be followed if you know that you can pull this off. It can be very tricky when you are not prepared with the subject at hand.

You might have to re-shoot some parts and will also have to rely on good editing to make good videos.

**Preparing a rough draft**: This style of presentation of vlogs is the one that is followed by most vloggers. It lies somewhere between the method where the vlogger prefers an extempore and the method where he prefers a well-rehearsed script.

The vlogger prepares a rough draft of what he will be speaking about once he decides to record the vlog. He makes sure that he has a coherent beginning, middle and the end. Even in this method, the vlogger relies on these mental notes that he makes. When he researches for the subject, he makes sure that he understands the subject well and also makes a lot of mental notes.

If there are some key points that the vlogger does not want to miss then he will make note of these key points in his rough draft. Make sure that you mention your key points clearly so that you have no trouble referring to them at a later stage.

This is a good way to start vlogging. This method will allow you to be spontaneous and will also help you to have the backup of the rough draft. The rough draft is like an assurance that the vlogger has that everything is under control.

This style is a highly preferred style because it takes the middle road and allows you to deviate to either side. You can have a control over your content and can still be spontaneous.

You should prepare a draft with some important notes and some statements that you would want to use in your video. It is important to have an idea what you will be speaking about and how long you would be speaking for. This means a lot of research and preparation will also go into this style of presentation of the videos.

You should select a subject and research exhaustively on the topic. It is important that when you decide to shoot the video, you have the draft for reference. You should have a lot of knowledge about the subject, no matter what the subject is. It is also important to be in tune with the latest developments in the subject. You can also rehearse with the rough draft before you are ready to shoot the video.

**Preparing a full draft:** As the name suggests, in this style of presentation, the presenter will prepare a full draft when he is researching for the subject. There are many successful vloggers that find this particular style of presentation the safest of all. There is a very little scope for error in this style of presentation. It should be noted that the amount of research and study that goes into preparing the video will be pretty much the same for all the three styles. You can't escape that, but you can choose a style that suits your personality the best.

The end aim should be to make videos that are loved by your audience. You should do all that is needed for doing so for your audience.

In comparison to the second style, in this style of presentation you will have to prepare the entire script from the beginning to the end. The script will be structured in a way that all the information that you wish to share if included in the same. While in the rough draft the vlogger prepares only a skeleton for reference, in this style the vlogger will know exactly what he will speak about in front of the camera.

Even the pauses are well planned. The jokes or punches that you will be using to make your vlog interesting are also planned and written in advance. The script or the full draft will not leave anything for the last minute. Everything will be planned well, though you can definitely make changes to your script if you think that something is not working well for you.

There are many people who complain that this style lacks the realism and spontaneity of the first two styles, but if you practice well then you can include spontaneity even with so much preparation.

You will have to work harder on your expressions and style of speaking, so that it does not look that you are just uttering some mugged up lines. You have to bring in some emotions when you speak. This will come with practice. So, the more you practice, the better you get at this.

The vloggers that focus on serious subjects that require too much research prefer this style of presentation. They find it easier to be well prepared before they shoot the video. And also, when you prepare a full draft, there is no chance that you will miss out any important piece of information.

If you are dealing with subjects that have too much information that needs to be shared then you should use this style. This will make sure that you are not missing any relevant information that the viewer needs to know.

If you find yourself being too confused regarding the style of presentation, then you can practice with all the three styles. This will help you to understand what style suits you the best.

You should not blindly follow what your favourite vlogger is doing. It is more important to be the best in your own style. But, before you are the best, you need to find your style. Practice and see what works best for you.

You can also shift from one style to another as per requirements of the vlog. Just be ready to experiment and adopt things that suit you the best. Even your favourite vlogger would have done the same. Nobody knows for sure unless and until they have made some trial and errors. Prepare yourself for this and enjoy this process of vlogging.

**Tips to prepare a great content script for your vlog**

You will have to mix and match and do what you like the best. While you are rehearsing and preparing for the script of your vlog, you would need many a tips. The following tips will surely help you to make great videos:

- You should be to the point. There is no point in beating around the bush. Nobody ever said that a 10 minute video is better than a 5 minute one. If you can finish in 5 minutes, you should do that. There is no point in wasting time.

- Don't blabber. You should only use coherent statements. It is very important that you make sense.

- Do your research well. When you will do your research well, you will automatically blabber less. You have to have some real researched content. Even if you will be sharing your opinions on the vlog, proper research should be done.

- It is extremely important that you value time. This means that you should value not just your time, but also the time of the viewer. Time should be an important factor when you are working on the content.

- While you are prepared well, you shouldn't sound like you have been rehearsing all day and night. It should look natural and easy.

- The language that you use should be simple. Everybody who knows the language should be able to follow you easily. Don't look for big words to make your script interesting. Unless you are doing a language tutorial, keep the language as simple as possible.

- You should keep an eye on what other vloggers of your genre are posting. This will help you to be up-to-date. You don't have to cheat or copy. You just need to know what is happening at their end.

- You should do what people like. Keep it simple for them. Understand what they like and use it in your videos. There is no point in working hard and presenting people with something that they don't appreciate.

- And last but not the least, always go with the flow. Do what seems and feels right. Great content is something that hits the right spots. Keep this in mind.

# Chapter 4: Building a brand

After you have decided the main theme and subject of your vlog, you have to plan on how to get the vlog started. If you think about this then you will understand that there might be hundreds of vlogs on the same theme as yours. You have to make your vlog your own.

It should be your personal identity. It needs to be different from all others on the Internet. It would not be just a platform for you to share your interests and thoughts. It'll be like a brand for you. You would be known by that brand. So, it is important that you create a brand that suits you and your personality. You should help to build a brand that has a strong brand recall value. This is the only way you can stay relevant. The viewers should be able to recognize your brand and associate it with you.

If you do a study of all the popular and successful vloggers, you will see that over time, these people have turned into self-sufficient media units. They operate and function in a way any media unit does. They have a brand name and a logo. They go all out to promote this brand name and logo.

A careful look at these vlogs will make you realize that a lot of thought has gone into its creation. You have to work hard on your videos. But, before you can do that you should give some thought to how you want to present yourself. How would you like your brand to be seen? What kind of a design would suit the basic theme of your vlog? How can the design help you to add more value to your vlog?

Success is not a phenomenon that will happen by chance. If there is no input, can you expect any kind of output? The vloggers that have made it to the top didn't do it by a fluke. While they have worked hard on the content of their vlog, they have also given importance to their brand value. There is some kind of uniformity or consistency that they have tried to maintain in their videos. Some of them present themselves in a certain way that it adds to their image.

Some of them try to keep the backdrop the same for all videos. Almost all of them have invested their thought in a good brand name and logo. This name and logo helps them to be more popular amongst the masses. They use these as signatures. Few of them get their merchandize done with the brand name and logo. In short, vlogging is much more than just shooting videos. It is a creation and maintenance of a certain brand.

If you have a logo for your vlog, it will be a like a stamp mark for you. You can stamp all your videos with this logo. This is a simple way to help people recognize you and your brand.

## 1. Building an image

It is important that you work on building a positive image for your viewers. People will judge you all the time. If you have not thought about how you want to appear in front of the camera, you will not be taken seriously.

If you are thinking that you'll vlog about unrelated things in a casual manner, without giving much thought to your image in front of the camera, then you are not going to go far. It is your vlog and you will be free to do all that you want. But, if you are looking at earning money and making a brand name, then there are many things you need to think about.

All the successful vloggers have worked on an image for themselves and their brands. If you closely observe, these vloggers keep certain things constant. They dress up a certain way. They use a certain kind of backdrops for their videos. They make sure that they don't deviate too far from their theme. This is important so that the viewer connects to you. If you keep everything random, the viewer will have a hard time connecting with you. Above all, you have to be presentable all the time. Be pleasant for the viewers. They are giving you their time, so you owe this to them.

A brand can only succeed if you are regular and consistent. If a brand decided to sell soap today, food tomorrow and clothes the day after, they will only lose trust with their customers. Even if you wish to expand, there is a place and time for that.

Before you put up your first video, work on what image you want to maintain. To gain the trust of your viewers, you have to be consistent. After watching a couple of your videos, they should begin to relate to you. Your personality and consistency will keep them hooked and your brand name and logo will help them to find you easily. Make sure that you are consistent with the various elements of your vlog.

You can always think of innovative ways to keep your brand name popular and relevant with time, but to begin with, work on the basics. Create a brand name, logo, theme and theme music. This will get you started.

## 2. Brand name

The first thing that comes to mind when thinking about building a brand is the brand name. Think if you had no name, how would people address you? A brand name is the first identity of your vlog.

43

When you are thinking of a brand name, remember that the name needs to catch the attention of a person. It should not be too long. People should be able to remember it and search for it easily. It should be very precise and direct. If you are a fashion blogger, think for a relevant name. Don't beat about the bush.

While it is important to have a good name, don't get all flustered for the same. The name should be creative, but don't get too overwhelmed. There are many vloggers who used their own names for their vlogs and are doing pretty good today.

A good name will not guarantee success to you. It will help your audience to relate to you. Try to name the vlog based on the main theme of the vlog. If you can't find anything that appeals to you, then you can also use your own name.

Another important point that you should note here is that you should finally choose the name that you can own over all platforms of social media. For example, you were able to select a certain name for yourself on YouTube, but when you looked for the same name on Twitter and Facebook, the name was taken. This can be a big problem for you.

Just imagine a viewer likes your video and decides to follow you on twitter and Facebook, but because the same name is owned by someone else on these platforms, you end up giving a follower to someone else. You could lose many such followers to someone like this. So, your aim should be to look for a name that you can solely own over the entire web.

You should make it a point to buy a website domain name. This will be helpful for you in future. When you start earning from your vlog, you would have to maintain a blog or website or both along with the vlog. This will help you to improve your earnings from your vlog.

You should always plan things keeping the long term plan in view. Though you might choose any name for your channel, it is better to choose a name that you can later use for your website name also. Make sure that the name is available.

You can trust websites such as bluehost.com and godaddy.com to check whether the name you want is taken away or is still available. If the name is already in use, then you have no other option but to look for another name. But, this initial hiccup in the beginning is better than bigger issues later. The last thing you want is to lose viewers and revenue to someone else because of a name. It is always better to use your brain and think of another name.

Some tips that will help you in selecting the right name for your vlog:

- The viewers might search you with the theme of your vlog. So, it could be a good idea to have the theme a part of the name. YouTube is owned by Google. So, if a viewer needs a certain kind of content, they will most probably search it on Google.

- If your brand name has the theme in the name, you could feature on the search list, which increases your chances of getting viewers. Of course, this should be done only if it fits well. There is no need to force the theme idea into the name of the vlog. The name should not look odd. It is more important for the name to be short and precise than have the entire theme idea.

- You need to think about the vlog in a long term way. If the vlog does very well and you become a rising star, how would you want to be recognized? People will remember the name of your vlog. Would you be comfortable if it is your name? You need to be sure of this. It is a personal decision, so it is better to think about this.

- Search for various vlogs that cater to your theme. You will find plenty of them. Now, pay attention to the names of these vlogs. Understand how the vlogger might have named the vlog. How can you be a little different? What can you do to catch the imagination of the viewer? Think about all these things and you might get an idea.

- Another important tip that you need to keep in mind is that your vlog name should not be very long. Imagine a viewer wants to search specifically for you. If you have a long name, it is a big problem for the viewer to remember and then eventually search for you online. Your brand name needs to be convenient and easy for the viewer also.

- Think of a few names and write them down. Ask your family and friends to vote for names that they think are the best of the entire lot. See which name gets the highest votes. This is a simple way to find a good name. You may even ask them to suggest a few names.

- You can also take help from some online sites that generate names. You will have to provide the theme and the website will mix and match various words and generate a name that suits the theme that you entered. An example of one such website is 'Bustname'.

## 3. Brand logo

The next important thing that will help you in building a brand is a brand logo. The brand logo is as important as the brand name, so equal importance should be given to the two. There are many popular brands. As a customer, the brand means quality and assurance to you. This is the importance of brand recall and brand consistency. Work on building both. You will be using your logo a lot, so it is only important that you pay enough attention to it.

To begin with, the logo should appeal to you. If decide a logo in hurry and later get bored of it, what's the use? If you keep changing the logo every month, can you think of making a positive impression of your viewers?

There must be some brand that you love. Just imagine that if the brand logo is changed every few months, wouldn't this amuse you? Wouldn't you lose trust in the brand? The same applies to your brand also. Take your time and come up with a logo that you like. It should be something that you will like even seven years from now.

The logo will appear on the very top of your vlog. It only makes sense that you make the logo as attractive as possible. Don't choose colours that irritate the eye. They should be pleasant to the eye.

It is important to work on the design of the logo. You can take inspiration from anywhere for the same. You can find an idea for the design in a magazine or on some billboard on the road.

You can also take inspiration from other vloggers. Understand the meaning of the brand logos of your favourite vloggers. This will help you understand what kind of thought process will help you to design an effective logo.

You should try to design a logo that sets you apart from the rest of the vloggers that create videos on the same theme as yours. Wouldn't you want to view the video of a vlogger who has an interesting logo? The logo could help you to attract more viewers on your vlog and the quality of your videos that keep them there.

**Types of logo:**

There are mainly three types of logos. When you are designing your logo, knowledge of these three types will help you to come up with something you want:

**- An icon:** You can use a symbol or icon as the logo of your channel. There are no letters or words in this kind of a logo. There are many big brands that go only with a symbol or icon. If you want to go for this kind of logo, then you will have to think about some unique icon that complements your vlog in some way. You can also use interesting doodles as icons. No matter what icon you choose, it is very important that it should have some meaning to your vlog. This is how the audience will relate to your logo.

**- A Word:** You can use letters or a word as the logo of your channel. You can choose certain abbreviations that explain something relevant to your vlog channel. This is a simple way of setting a logo for your vlog. But, if this suits you well then you should go for it. But, again the letters that you choose should have some relevance to your vlog channel. You can get creative and try out different fonts and letter styles if you go for this type of logo design.

**- A Combination of icon and word or letter:** the third type of logo is where a combination of the first two is used. You can have a symbol and letter or word to go with this. This is the most popular of all the three styles of logo designing. YouTube and other big brands use this kind of style. Many popular vloggers have also chosen this as their style of logo.

It is very important to give a good thought to your logo. You should design it well and should pay equal importance to all the elements related to the brand logo. If you are looking for some advice to design the logo in an appropriate way, then the following tips will be useful for you:

- You should go for a style that is not too cumbersome and complicated. It should be easy to recognize and understand. A logo should help you to create a value and not complicate people. It should be fun, meaningful and relevant to your vlog.

- You should make sure that you choose the right colours for your brand logo. The viewer should be able to relate the colour to your vlog. For example, as a viewer you might instantly relate red and black to YouTube. Make sure the colours are not painfully bright.

- You can choose a combination of colours or a single colour. You should try to avoid using too many colours. It will only lead to a complicated and messy look.

- You need to choose the right font for your letters. Make sure that the style you choose complements your vlog. For example, if your vlog is fashion related, you can go for funky styles. If it is a serious blog, you should be choosing the font accordingly.

- Your target audience can also help you in choosing a good font. For example, if you are looking at young viewers, then a suitable funky style will appeal to them. These are small things, but they will add up to make your vlog attractive.

- It is important that you understand the regulations that Google implies on the uploading of images in the logo.

- If you think that you are unable to design a suitable and good logo for your vlog even after multiple trials, then it is always suitable to go for professional help. You can look for logo designers online. Make sure that you go through your professional designer's previous designs before hiring him.

Let him know your requirements and ideas to help him design something that you like. You will be able to find such services for as low as 5 dollars.

You should spend some time to understand the kind of logo that will suit your vlog. It is important that the icon represents you, your personality and your vlog. Don't go for a logo only because it looks good. It should have some relevance to the work that you do.

### 4. Brand theme song

Another aspect of building a good brand is to have a brand song. It will make your vlog easily recognisable. Many brands have theme songs. You might even recognize the theme of a particular brand even if it is playing in some other room.

Most of the popular and high-earning brands have a theme song. This song is like an identity for them. Everything that you will choose for your brand will become its face and identity. So, it is only important that you choose things that will have some meaning even ten years from now.

The theme song should be catchy and should be something that makes a strong hold on the imagination of the listener. It should do justice to your vlog. The song will play in the beginning of each video, so it is important that it is good. The last thing you want is annoying your viewers because of a bad theme song.

There are many ways to choose a theme song for your channel or vlog. If you have a passion in music, then you can create something on your own. But, this is absolutely optional. You should be fine even if you don't know how to create music. An important point that you need to note here is that you can't just copy any song from anywhere. It will violate the copyright rules of the song.

You should be aware of the rules before you can use any song or tune for your vlog. Many people commit this mistake of just copying a song and remixing it a bit. This will only lead to legal actions against them because of copyright infringement. Make sure that you don't fall prey to this.

You will benefit in knowing that YouTube has its own audio library that allows you to use the songs included in the library.

You should a little research before you finalize a theme song for your channel. Don't just use the very first song you listen to. Listen to a few theme songs and understand what you like. You need to be sure before you zero in on any theme song.

## 5. Selecting the right location

Another important part of your brand building is selecting the right location to shoot your videos. Would you like to watch a channel where the vlogger sits in an unhygienic environment with filth all around? Nobody would want to waste their time on a vlogger who does not even the take the efforts to keep the surroundings right.

You don't have to book a fancy villa to shoot your videos. You can do with whatever you have. But there are a basic points that you need to keep in mind. It is very important that you keep the surroundings clean. There should be no piles of books or clothes lying around. Make the place neat as if a guest is visiting you.

The backdrop that you choose should be easy on the eyes. Don't go for something that is too over the top. The idea is to be subtle yet classy. If you over do, it will only hamper the overall effect. The vibe of the location should be very chilled out and positive. The viewer should fall in love with what they see on the screen. This will only add to the viewership of your vlog.

If you are shooting in your room, you can put a nice painting on the wall. But, it should not be too distracting. Just keep the things simple and tidy. You can use good lights to add to the effect. Also, it is important to keep shifting locations. If you have a traveling vlog, then you have to. But, otherwise you should try to maintain a consistency even in the locations in your vlog.

## Putting your best foot forward

You are also a part of your brand. The way you present yourself will also add or take away from your brand. So, it is more than important to put your best foot forward. Vlogging will help you not just to gain popularity and money, but also to create a new image yourself. You will be able to look at yourself in a new way and will be able to discover new things about you.

You would be shocked to know that most successful vloggers were not the same personality wise in the beginning of their careers. Many of them have confessed to be going through personality issues, such as low confidence.

Vlogging helped them to reinvent and get a new confidence. If they can do it, so can you. So, irrespective of how you look or behave right now, you can still be a totally different person when you vlog. Even if you are struggling with confidence issues, you can be one of the best vloggers.

The vlogging business gives you an opportunity to improve on any bit that you think has not gone right. You can always reshoot and edit and make your videos perfect. You don't have to shoot everything in one go.

When you upload the video and see people taking positively to your personality and hard work, it will only help you to gain confidence and get better. Confidence is the key to many a locks. Once you are confident of what you are doing, you will only get better at it.

When you vlog, you will notice some amazing changes in yourself. Vlogging will bring a positive change in your personality. You have the opportunity to choose a personality and style that you wish the world to see. People will start recognising your style. This will increase your confidence as a person and also as an artist. This will only motivate you to create better content for your audience.

The next chapter is fully dedicated to help you build an image that will suit your vlog. This is called your camera persona. You will be able to learn tips and tricks to be the best version of yourself in front of the camera.

If you are someone who is not naturally very comfortable in front of the camera, then you need to work harder. But, this is no way means that you can't be good at it. You will learn the tricks just like everybody else does. You will learn that with practice you can also have an appealing personality like all those popular and rich vloggers.

# Chapter 5: Shooting and editing the videos

As a beginner, you shouldn't waste your time and energy on looking for ideas for the best camera. There is no need to do an in depth study of the best cameras available on the market. The best of vloggers also started at a very basic level. They made use of the best that they had.

You don't need to spend a fortune in buying the best camera in the country. This will not add to your vlogging. As a novice, there are other things that you must be concentrating on. Even your favourite vlogger started with a pretty basic camera. You can move to better ones as you progress in your journey as a vlogger. You will get plenty of time for that.

A basic idea about the equipment will help you to be better prepared. It is important that you learn to use the basic stuff in the best possible way, rather than buying the best stuff and then struggle to use it. You can always upgrade whenever you feel like.

If you are looking at cost effective ways to make videos, then this chapter can help you. You will learn about the bare minimum that you need to shoot a video for your vlog. You will learn about some simple ways to shoot good quality videos.

If you wish to start as a vlogger, the basic equipment that you should be looking at getting for yourself includes the follows:

-   Camera which can record videos for you
-   Microphone
-   Lighting
-   Editing software

As a beginner, you could be concerned about the money that you might have to invest in the vlogging business. Nobody wants to invest without really having a certainty that they will earn more than they spend. This is a crucial time for you when you are learning the very basics of vlogging. There is no need to make an investment that you regret later.

You can do pretty well with the most basic stuff that you might even have at your home. You should aim at using these things to the best of your advantage. Learn the know-how of all these things to avoid making any mistakes.

## 1. Camera

The one thing that you can't do without as a vlogger is a camera. You should get a camera that can record videos. Now, you need to make sure that the camera is capable of focussing well; else the picture will not be clear. As a vlogger, you should get clear and well-focussed images because nobody will waste time on a badly shot video.

Most cameras today will help you with this. If you already have a camera, then you are good to go. If you wish to buy one, then just get a good camera with a good pixel quality. Before you buy the camera, make sure that you are comfortable with the camera. Try using it and make sure that it is the one you need.

You can also buy a good tripod stand for the camera. This is not a necessity, but the tripod stand will help you to keep the camera steady. If the camera is not steady, you can expect a shaky video. A shaky and badly shot video will end your vlogging career even before it is started.

Another option is to use the webcam of your laptop. If your laptop has a decent webcam, you are good too go. You can try recording a few videos with your laptop webcam. If the images are clear, then you can use the same. You should make sure that the images are not blurry.

Many vloggers prefer to shoot with the webcam in the beginning. It is only later that they graduate to better cameras. In the beginning, you just need a well shot video from a decent camera.

## 2. Lighting

This is another concern for a vlogger looking to shoot good quality videos. To understand how important lighting is for the shooting videos, do a simple experiment. Shoot a video in the open where the sun is bright. Once you have done that, go inside and put all the curtains. Now shoot another video in the dim light that you are getting. Don't use any additional source of light.

After you have shot the video, you should watch both the videos and compare the two. You will understand the importance of good lighting for shooting a video. A good light will bring out the best of everything that is being shot. In a bad light, the camera will not focus well. This will result in poor quality images. You will have to strain your eyes to watch the video. This is something that you wouldn't want. You would only want to shoot the very best videos for the viewers who will invest their time in viewing.

## 3. Microphone

You will definitely need a microphone to record the videos of your vlog. There are many kinds of microphones available on the market. In the beginning, don't worry about all this.

You can always get a better microphone at a later stage if need be. To begin with, there are many cheap options that you can look at.

Many vloggers make use of the microphone of their laptops. They use the webcam and the microphone of the laptop to shoot their videos. This is a very simple way to make videos. You can also use the laptop to make the videos.

If you are looking at other options, then there are many for you. There are many simple microphones available that are usb compatible. You can use such microphones in combination with the laptop webcam. You will be able to buy cheap microphones very easily.

It is always advisable to test the microphones before you buy them. It would be great if you can test the microphone in combination with the camera that you intend to use.

The basic aim of the microphone is to record the sounds and voices. It should be able to do it well. You might have seen videos where the sound appears a little out of sync and disturbed. You should avoid making this mistake. It is important to make videos with clear sound. Even if you have shot the best video, bad sound quality is enough to ruin it for you.

It is quite easy to test a microphone for use. Firstly, you should check the kind of sound the microphone captures when there is no sound. If there is a buzz at this time, then there is nothing to worry about. This can be completely covered when you are editing your video in the end.

Secondly, you should say something and see how well your voice is captured. A bad microphone will make you sound very bad. The voice will sound extremely dry and harsh. It is important to avoid such kind of microphones.

Even if you are looking to buy something cheap, don't compromise on the quality. The microphone should be able to capture sound well and should make you sound like you. As your personal journey as a vlogger progresses, you should look at buying a good microphone with good directional sensors. These sensors capture the sound well. While they capture even the faintest noises, they don't emit a buzz when there is no sound to be captured.

## 4. Shooting the video

You must be dreaming of making millions with the popularity of your vlog. But, to get to that point, you have to keep all the basics right. Once you are ready with your equipment, the theme of the vlog, you have to work on the content of the video that you plan to shoot. After that you have to shoot the videos. This is something that you will improve with time.

As and when you make more and more videos, you will get better acquainted with everything related to your vlog, be it shooting videos or improvising your content. But, even in the beginning, there are a few things that you need to keep in mind. These simple tips and tricks will help you to get the kind of videos you have been hoping to get.

- It is important to place the camera at the right place. If the camera is placed in the wrong direction, you can't hope to make a great video, in spite of all the efforts you put.

- The simple tip that you need to remember all the time is that the camera needs to be placed at a higher level as compared to you. The camera needs to look down upon you. You can also keep the camera at the same level as you.

- The idea is to give the camera your best profile. If you place the camera in such a way that it looks upward when shooting you, the video wouldn't be that great. The camera will be unable to capture your best profile hence leading to a poor quality video.

- If you want to look straight into the camera while speaking and shooting the vlog, you should position the camera in a way that it is a fixed height as you on the wall opposite to you. This is the best way to do it.

- There are some people that place the camera on one side. The camera shoots in a diagonal way. This is not a great angle for the camera. The backdrop and the entire video will look a little untidy like this.

- These are very simple tips and are also very easy to follow. But, when you follow them, you make sure that your videos are shot in the most professional way even with the most basic of equipment.

- When you have set the camera, you need to make use of the lighting sources that are available with you. As stated earlier, you can do very well with the most basic sources of light. You just need to use them in the right way to be able to shoot good quality videos.

- When you are setting your light source, make sure that there is some light source at the back of the camera. This source of light should be throwing light at you from that position. You could make use of a tube light or a desk lamp to throw light from behind the camera at you. This light will make you the focus of the camera. While the backdrop will also be covered by the camera, the light will help to enhance your features. It will establish you as the main focus of the video.

- This light should be enough to bring you at the spot light, but if you feel that you need more depth, you can use another light source. It is important to place this light source in the right direction. You should keep the light source at a nine o'clock position in the direction where you are facing the camera.

- To bring in more layers into the look, you should make sure that the second light source which is kept at the nine o'clock position should be less in terms of intensity of the light when compared to the main light source that is behind the camera.

- You should try with both the light sources placed in their ideal spots. You should use both if you like the effect or the first one if you find that better. These simple tips and tricks will help you to add more depth to your personality and in turn will help you to shoot better videos for your vlog.

- A good lighting effect can actually help you to make your videos as professional as possible. If you understand how it works in your favour, you can bring in a great deal of difference to your videos. You can immediately get into the bunch of vloggers who are professionals. It helps to establish that this is not just your hobby but you are pretty serious about the same.

- Another simple trick that can help you further enhance the quality of your videos is to use another light source. This light source will be behind you. The main light coming from behind the camera and this light should not clash with each other because if this happens then you will go completely out of focus.

- To make sure that this extra light adds more to the video and particularly to your profile; you should use a rather dim light source in comparison to the main light. Another point that needs to be remembered here is that you should be exactly in front of the light so that no clash happens. The soft light from behind you will help to bring more depth to the entire look. You should definitely try this trick. This will help you to shoot even better videos than you had ever imagined.

- Another trick to add different kinds of desired effects in your videos is to use coloured lights. You don't have to spend any extra money to buy these lights. All you need to do is buy some coloured translucent sheets. These translucent sheets are easily available at any stationary shop.

- There are many colours from which you can choose the ones that you need. Just fix the coloured sheet over the light source with the help of cellotapes. This will help you to get coloured light.

- Work with the lights. Use these tricks and shoot some practice videos. Look at the videos and understand what you could have done better. This will help you to become a pro with your equipment in the shortest possible time. You should understand that even if you get the best equipment, you will waste it if you don't understand the basics.

- You need to be absolutely clear about these simple things if you want to make great videos. Great videos are made by understanding the basics and using them to your advantage. So, instead of running after high end equipment, try to make the best of what is readily available to you in your home. This is the secret to great videos.

**The background and the foreground**

When you are shooting a video, the foreground and the background also play a very important role in your shot. If you view from the eye of the camera, the frame that is captured has two parts, the background and the foreground. If you are shooting in your room, then the wall will act as the background.

You might not realize but the choice of a good background also adds or takes away from a video. The background should be bright, but should not be so loud that it takes away from the main action happening. If the wall is serving as the background then you can put a beautiful painting on the wall to add to the effect.

You can also use various hangings to make it more beautiful. Remember not to go overboard because that will make the background very distracting, and this is the last thing that you would want.

You will be standing in front of the background. It is very important that you focus on keeping yourself better focussed for the camera. It has already been discussed that this can be easily done by use the right light sources at the right places.

While it is important not to give the background undue importance, it is important to give it the right importance. If you keep the background too dull, then this will not look good in the video. A bright background is always preferred. You can experiment with different backgrounds. You can also view the usual backgrounds of various vloggers.

As a viewer, you will notice that a dull background dampens the overall mood of the video. On the other hand, a bright background adds to the positive vibe of the video. You should keep these points in mind when finalizing the background of the video.

You don't need to be an expert in videography when it comes to shooting for vlogs. But, it will always help you if you have some basic knowledge. You should understand why a camera is placed where it is placed. You should understand the importance of light sources and the background in the video.

You should also understand how to focus on the foreground and how to use the background in the right way. When you are ready to take a shot, the rule of three will come to your rescue. According to this rule of videography, the screen or the frame is equally divided into 9 parts or sections (3X3).

There are few interest points in the frame that are most focussed. According to the rule, a point where of these nine sections intersect is an interest point. The entire frame will automatically have many interest points. It is important that the area that needs the most focus is within the frames of these points. This will help to keep that area in maximum focus.

During the shooting of the video, you should make sure that your eyes are under proper focus. They should be under the frame of the points. This will bring the right focus at the area where you want it. It should also be noted that if you are not the object of focus, then there is something substantial in the frame.

It should be noted when you keep these intersecting points free and empty, it affects the video on the whole. You will notice a dull and lethargic look to the video. Make sure that you make use of this simple tip right from your first video.

**Screen capture software**

Screen capture software does exactly what it says: it captures or records everything that you do on your computer screen. Depending on what type of vlogger you want to be, this might come in handy.

- Jing www.techsmith.com/jing.html

- Camstudio www.camstudio.org

- ScreenCastOMatic www.screencast-o-matic.com.

- Small Video Soft www.smallvideosoft.com/screen-video-capture

- Techsmith www.techsmith.com/camtasia.html

- Jing www.jingproject.com

- Viddler www.viddler.com

- EZS www.EZS3.com

## 5. Editing

When you become a vlogger, you actually decide to be a one man army. You will be the cameraman, the presenter, the producer, the director and the editor. While this might look very exhaustive to some people, it actually gives you a lot of freedom to do whatever you want to.

If you can channel your energy and all your resources in the right direction, you will actually enjoy this process of getting too much in limited time and resources.

As the vlogger, you have the freedom to shoot and re-shoot your videos as many times you want. If you are not happy with the outcome, then you can decide to take another shot. Another interesting thing that helps to make videos entertaining is editing.

You can edit videos to chop off parts you don't like. If you learn to edit well, you can use this tool to make your videos more fun and concise.

There are many people out there who believe that only good content is required to make your video a hit. Try taking the best content and present it in a poor way with no lighting effects and zero editing. Your video will be a big flop.

Viewers want everything. They want good content, good presentation, great videos and excellent editing. The audience expects so much because there are some great vloggers out there who are already providing all this and more to the audience. Why would the audience settle for less?

If you wish to succeed and make it to the top charts of the vloggers, then it is better to make a note of all these very important points. You can get there sooner if you decide to master the most important tools in the very beginning. After your video has been shot the way you wanted to shoot it, get on a mission to edit it well. Make it presentable and enjoyable for the viewer. If you learn the basics, editing can be one of your most important tools as a vlogger.

When you edit your videos, the editing software will provide you with many options to make your video better. While it is important to edit well, it is also important to not get carried away. Many new vloggers commit this mistake of getting overwhelmed with all that they can do with their videos. They try and use too many transitions and effects in their videos.

You should understand that excess of anything can be bad, even editing. You have to know how far to go and when to stop. This knowledge will come only with time, but as a rule, remember not to use too many effects and transitions. Avoid committing this mistake right from the very beginning.

**Need to edit**

It is important that you understand the importance of editing in a vlogger's life. How can an edit help improve your videos? This is a question that will pop in your head every time someone says that editing can help to improve the quality of your videos.

This section will help you to understand the importance of editing in vlogging. You will be able to appreciate its need and importance. The following tips will help you to know why editing is important:

Audiences have a very limited attention span. You can't make them sit and listen to you, while you talk for hours. You have to tweak your videos according to the needs of the audience. When you edit a video you make sure that the video caters to the needs of the audience.

- The effects that you can add to your videos with the help of editing will help you to make your videos more entertaining. There are many kinds of effects that you can use. It is important that you don't use all the effects at the same time.

Use them according to your requirements as a vlogger. If used in the right way, these effects can enhance the overall look of the videos. They make the videos more pleasing and pleasant. Your audience will also love to watch such videos.

- Sometimes, when you shoot a video, you don't realize the overall impact that the video will have. You think that you have shot the best video ever. It's only when you go back to the video that you realize that certain parts were unnecessary.

There is no need to re-shoot the entire video again. You can simply edit out the parts that you think are superfluous and are not adding anything to the video.

- It is during the editing phase that you can add good music to your videos. The quality of any video can be enhanced by the addition of music. You can choose suitable background music for your video.

**Editing software**

Another essential for budding vloggers is the editing software. You just can't shoot and upload whatever you have shot. You will have to edit many parts of the video that you wish to upload. Editing will help you improve the overall quality of the video. The video will come crisper and better.

These days, most laptops come with in-built editing software. You can make use of this software to edit your videos. This in-built software will give you some important and basic tools that should be enough for you to edit your videos, at least in the beginning.

If you are looking for another option or if your laptop does not have the software, then you can easily download editing software from the web. There are many editing softwares that are available free of cost. You can just download them and start using them.

There are many others that have made their trial versions free. You can download the trial version and make use of it to edit the videos in the beginning of your career.

If you decide to use the trial version, then you should understand that the company will force you to buy the software. It might stamp or put a water-mark over your video. This is done so that you buy from them to get rid of the mark. It is always better to use the free software if you are unable to find a good trial version.

Editing software will help you to make your videos more presentable. An entire chapter has been dedicated to editing of videos in this book. It is not a rule to edit before you can upload. Nobody is going to stop you if you do so.

But, that could mean that your video is lacking in some aspect. If you can edit well, you can actually raise the standard of your video. This means that there are chances that more people will view it. This also means that you will be able to increase your revenue.

Spend some time in learning the tricks of good editing and understand the importance of good editing. All the top class vloggers make it a point to edit well before they upload the videos for the viewers. There are many vloggers who are very popular for their professional level editing.

You can start out on a basic level, but as you proceed in your vlogging journey, make it a point to pay more attention to this aspect of vlogging because it will help you to make better quality videos.

Here is a list of video editing software. These were all free at the time of writing this book.

- Avidemux

- Black Magic DaVinci Resolve

- Blender

- Hitfilm 4 Express

- Lightworks

- VSDC Free Editor

- YouTube Video Editor

Here is a list of video editing software, not free:

- Adobe After Effects

- Camtasia Studio

- Corel VideoStudio

- Cyberlink Power Director

- Edius

- Magic Movie Edit Pro

- Pinaccle Studio

- Final Cut Pro

- Imovie www.apple.com/mac/imovie

- Avidemux www.avidemux.sourceforge.net/

Please note you will have to check which software listed above is suitable for Windows and/or Mac/Apple computer.

## Converting Videos

You will probably need this type of software at some point. Your video might be too large to upload on certain sites or if you want to convert from a .movie format to an MP$; converting software will do this for you.

- Handbrake www.handbrake.fr

- YouConvertit www.youconvertit.com

- Zamzar www.zamzar.com

## 6. Using the right equipment

It is important that you look for the right equipment for shooting your videos. A stated earlier, you can start at a pretty basic level. You can shoot good quality videos even with your laptop camera and microphone. You can venture out into better stuff later on.

But, if you are looking for specific information on the right equipment for your vlog, then this section can guide you. You will be able to learn where to invest your money and time for better results.

## Cameras

Anybody with a blog that has video content is probably going to consider what the best camera is to create your content with. However, the best camera depends on what you're using it for. The perfect decision relies upon individual budgets as well as individual necessities.

Therefore, what may be a perfect answer for you won't be the best for another blogger! The uplifting news is that there are various options for a wide range of budgets and you can be guaranteed that you will find something that fits you perfectly.

-DSLRs have the finest adaptability with regards to capturing both photographs & video. If you want to incorporate both videos and still images in your blog, it is important to pick a camera that does both to a high standard.

- Action cams are the ideal fit for bloggers who are vlogging on the move, whether it be traveling around the world or merely taking your viewers to the supermarket.

- Cameras that use interchangeable lenses are not for the faint hearted. If you're an amateur, stick to something straightforward and reasonable before putting resources into costly hardware that you won't require or utilize.

- Make sense of your requirements first. Contingent upon the sort of shooting you'll be doing, you may require tripods, a camera with low-light recording capacities, or improved sound. Really think about how you need to utilize video to improve your blog first, and then start to think about the best camera to suit your needs.

Below are a few options to suit all types of vloggers:

**Smartphones**

There is no harm in utilizing your Smartphones & iPods for vlogging. As a matter of fact, cutting-edge Smartphones, iPods, and comparative gadgets can create amazing videos and rival most conventional cameras. Some of the best smartphones to use include:

-   The Apple iPod Touch fifth Gen
-   Apple iPhone
-   Google Nexus 7

**Simple Cameras**

The YouTube channel DailyTekk suggests that the best entry level cameras are:

**-Canon power shot g7x:** This camera is mostly suited to those who daily vlog. Famous vlogger AlfieDeyes of Pointlessblog uses this camera every day. It has a screen on the back that flips up so you can see yourself and a touch screen so can easily zoom in for close ups.

**- Sony cyber-shot rx100:** This camera also has the flip up screen. It is good in low light and has a compact size, so it is easy to carry around. It has a longer battery life than g7x and also has built in Wi-Fi. However, this camera is much more expensive than the g7x.

**- Gopro HERO4 Black:** This particular camera is favoured by vloggers covering sports events and those trying to be more creative with their set up. It captures wide angles and time lapse modes and shoots in 4k. It has a better microphone for vloggers moving around and on the go. It also has very good durability, so you can take it on a rugged terrain.

- **Samsung NX Mini:** This camera has all of the same features as the rx100 but it is much cheaper and smaller.

## Lights

### Ring lights

You need to make sure you purchase a few extra lights for your room so your face and body are well lit. Darkness is unflattering. Beauty vloggers tend to do a lot of close ups, so they just use one light source, which tends to be a ring light.

A Ring light is a hollow circle of light, within which your camera sits. You can always tell when a blogger is using a ring light, because it creates a ring reflection in the iris of their eyes. Lilly Pebbles, a popular YouTube Star, says she likes the ring light because it is small and easy to move around.

You don't need an expensive one; you just need a ring light that specifies its set to 5500k or 6500k. This means the ring mimics natural light as opposed to giving a yellowish or beige tinge. Amazon and eBay sell them for around £100.

### Three point lighting

If you are going to be far away from the camera or moving around, you will need lots of different lights to illuminate different parts of your body. This is known as three-point lighting. This is a way of reminding you to place your lights in a triangle around the set. You need to place one on each side and one in front of you.

### Soft box

You could also use a soft box, which diffuses light by bouncing it off of another light source (usually white or silver fabric). This is very flattering and helps to eliminate shadows.

For more information about the lighting to use, see videos by ItsJudyTime, DFWBeauty and Mei Mei makeup.

### Sound

Now that you've worked out how to look the best on screen with your camera and lighting, make sure your audience can hear you! What is the fun of a great video if it has a terrible sound?

The quality of the microphone on most of the cameras discussed above is adequate, but you might need extra microphones for shooting outside. Wind or traffic noises can interfere with the sound on most inbuilt cameras, so you may need to purchase extra microphones in this case.

The popular vlogging website vloggerpro.com recommends using Zoom H1 portable audio device to start out, because it is relatively low in price but still has impressive abilities. This is currently priced at 89 euros on amazon and it will make your videos a lot more professional.

You could also invest in a lapel mic (also known as lavaliermic). These kinds of mics can be clipped on to your clothing and have a belt pack that can be stored in your pocket. This makes them easier to use.

It is also important to note that the pack is battery powered, so you need to make sure you always have batteries to hand. These microphones are available for prices as low as 40 euros on amazon but will also sound very professional.

In spite of the fact that vlogging has only become more popular over the past couple of years, many people are still new to the universe of vlogging and don't yet realize what vlog or vlogging implies.

Vlogging is becoming more 'normal' and widespread, as camera equipment becomes distinctly less expensive and supporting programming & hosting, in addition to conglomeration, sites become more predominant.

Both Yahoo & Google include video segments and numerous MP3 players, such as 'bolster video'. Anybody with access to a video-capable camera and a moderately new PC with a high-speed connection can make a vlog and distribute it on the web. Here are a few ways you can share your videos:

- Create your video with your camera & save it as a recording on your PC. You can utilize effectively accessible software, such as QuickTime, Windows Movie Maker or iMovie (for Apple systems).

- Compact your video file. If you are looking for software to do so, then iMovie, Movie Maker, Avid Free DV and Final Cut Pro are among the software you can utilize.

- You should set up a blog. Feedburner and Blogger.com are prominent blog hosting sites.

- Make a screen grab of a picture from your video to show in your blog as the thumbnail.

- Get your real video content distributed on the web. There are a few open hosting services. BlipTV, Web Archive and OurMedia are open hosting services.

-Acquire an RSS channel with enclosures. You should also distribute your blog at Feedburner or a comparative webpage.

The vlogosphere is an extremely popularity based field. Unlike the predominant press, for example, TV or commercial Websites, vlogs are not, generally, made for profit.

Accordingly, vloggers are allowed to make their content about whatever they want, regardless of how questionable or obscure the theme. Vlogging furnishes a normal group of people and an opportunity to make their voices heard.

# Chapter 6: Using Photographs

You might want to add some photographs in your video, when you are editing the video or you might want to use photographs on your website. It is important for you to know that, in contradiction to common believe, that you can just take "any" picture from "any" website and use it as your own. An important word of warning is in place here:

Free is nice, we all like free stuff but free from the Internet sometimes comes with spyware, ads or SPAM e-mails. Some people will download anything without thinking about it first. Be VERY careful if you download anything from any website you haven't used before. It is *your* responsibility to check out that what you are downloading is trustworthy.

There are thousands of websites pretending to give you a solution to your problem when you download things, whilst they don't tell you that you are also downloading a virus or spyware to your computer. It can take you days to get the spyware or virus off your computer!

On top of that, most of the time the free anti spyware programs don't get rid of the serious spyware and you'll have to spend money on professional spyware software. Make sure you search thoroughly for "xyz + review" or "xyz + scam", etc... before using new tools.

**Very important to mention:** While some image sites are perfectly safe, others may be compromised or infected with spyware, malware, or adware. A site that is currently safe to use may not be days, weeks, months, or even years from now.

### The Dangers of Stealing Online Photos
Just because it is on the Internet does not mean you can use it and the term royalty free does not mean it is free to use. Images that you find via a search in Google are almost always copyrighted, so you can't just use them on your blog or website.

Visitor's eyes are often drawn to the images on your website so it's important to place an image, a visual that illustrates your point. Important: always check, whichever website you use to obtain images, that you credit the image, if required to do so.

Downloading copyrighted photos from the Internet without authorisation from their photographers or original publishers is risky and can lead to adverse consequences if these pictures are found in your creations. This is especially true if you use stolen images for commercial purposes. There are software tools, such as TinEye and Google "Search by Image" that can find duplications of images.

Ever since you were in school, you were assigned to write reports requiring some degree of research. Your teachers told you that plagiarism is wrong and a violation of copyright.

Like most creators, you want to complete your project and get it up and running TODAY! If you're one of those people, you need some images NOW! Hence, you may be more than willing to just steal the images and take the risks that come with it. In this great big world of exponential online growth, some may assume that their odds of getting caught are extremely slim, like a million to one. Some who have websites or blogs online may have the attitude, "It'll never happen to me!" Well, think again, as it happened to me.

---

**Most important lessons for you to remember:**

1) Don't steal photos - EVER.

2) Don't accept photos from other people. YOU are responsible if the photo is on YOUR website.

3) ALWAYS check the terms and conditions when you use a royalty free photo (free or payable)

---

### Get free images online

Here are some sites where you can download images for free BUT you still need to check each image for the terms and conditions in which you can use the images e.g. some are for commercial use, other aren't. It is always a good idea to refer to the source of the image e.g. by putting the source underneath the image.

- Creative Commons www.search.creativecommons.org

 - Flickr www.flickr.com

- Getty Images www.gettyimages.co.uk

- Wikipedia Commons www.commons.wikimedia.org

There are A LOT more image sites, just search for "royalty free images".

## Get payable online

Here are some payable sites where you can buy images. These sites are called "stock photo"sites, so you can search for more sites.

- Fotolia www.fotolia.com

- Dreamstime www.dreamstime.com

- 123rf www.123rf.com

- Dollar Photo Club www.dollarphotoclub.com

- Big Stock Photo www.bigstockphoto.com

- Graphic Stock www.graphicstock.com

- Stock Pholio www.stockpholio.com

- Shutterstock www.shutterstock.com

- Istock Photo www.istockphoto.com

- Deposit Photo www.depositphoto.com

## Get icons and buttons online

If you are ever in need of an icon or a button, you can get them from these sites:

Icon Finder www.iconfinder.com

Find Icons www.findicons.com

Buttonland www.buttonland.com

## Editing images

The purpose of using imaging software is to adapt the image to your needs. The most common things you will do with images is cropping, resizing, changing file size and making thumbnails. Thumbnails are useful to link to full size images. You could use the full size image on your page and use the web design software to have the image fit the location. However, doing so would require the full file to load. A smaller thumbnail would load faster and the full file would only load if someone clicked on the thumbnail to see the full image. Imaging software can also do other tasks but altering an image, replacing elements or adding to them could be considered creating a derivative, which would require an authorisation.

Making a thumbnail could not be easier than with www.MakeAThumbnail.com. You can import a graphic and choose to make a thumbnail of that image and save it as a Jpeg.

Photoshop is generally known to be very good software to edit photographs but it is expense. Here are some alternatives:

The most widely used alternative to Photoshop is a program called GNU Image Manipulation Program or GIMP for short. It is an open source program (meaning everybody can use it) developed with a Creative Commons license. That means that it is free.

- The official site for GIMP is www.gimp.org

- A slightly different interface, one very similar to Photoshop, is available from the website www.gimpshop.com

Picmonkey www.picmonkey.com

- The second most popular alternative is Paint.net, available from the website www.getpaint.net This program does not have all the features of GIMP, however it does have all the features you are most likely to use. It is a good tool for those who have no experience with graphics.

- BeFunky www.befunky.com Some call it the world's best photo editor

- Pixlr at www.pixlr.com has levels for beginners, intermediate and advance users. It is a browser-based editor.

- Canva www.canva.com Create free designs without possessing any design skills. They also have lots of templates for social media use. Search for a photo or graphic and then use Canva to create a new design.

- Timeline Slicer www.timelineslicer.com is a cool tool to design images for your Facebook Profile or Page.

- Another great online graphics creator is Sumopaint. Download it free from www.sumoware.com. They also have a paid version but I am sure you can create some great things with the free version.

- Photovisi www.photovisi.com No need to create an account. This is a photo collage tool that is easy to use.

- TinyPNG www.tinypng.com Shrink PNG files. High resolution images can slow down your website. You can convert them to a smaller size.

# Chapter 7: How will you earn money from the vlog?

When you start vlogging, there are many questions that haunt you. Will you earn money through this? How much money can you expect to earn? How soon can you expect to earn the money? Can this be your full time job? How can you increase your chances to earn money through your vlog. All these are very legitimate questions that any vlogger will have.

You might have read many stories of how many vloggers make millions just through vlogging. But, when you read such stories, it is also important to dig deep into what lies within. How did these vloggers reach the point where they are today? How much did they earn in the beginning? What were the roadblocks the pitfalls that they faced in their journey?

It is only when you understand all these important points will you able to understand what you and expect from your vlog channel. It always pays to be as realistic as possible. Know where you stand and where you are headed.

It should also be noted here that you will see all kinds of examples in the vlogging world. You will find people who are vlogging full time, and then there are people who struggle to get even a few likes. There is something right that the successful ones must be doing and something wrong that the strugglers might be doing. It is important to have a realistic approach when you take to vlogging. This is not meant to scare you.

You probably know about the YouTube giants Jenna Marbles, PewDiePie and Zoella. Maybe they have inspired you in your pursuit of vlogging. You want to make it big like them. You want to have millions of followers like them. It is great to be inspired by these giants. However, what about all the smaller vloggers who make up a large sum of the content produced on YouTube? There are many more vloggers that you might know about.

While the popular ones get to make a living out of vlogging, the smaller vloggers have different challenges. A vlogger such as Zoella can create a fortune out of vlogging, but there are many others who are still struggling to get there.

Smaller channels more often than not don't make their living creating content. YouTube is merely something they do as a hobby as well as college or work.

The main idea is only to give you the right picture so that you can have a realistic approach towards the vlogging business. Don't expect to earn millions and billions from your first video. If you are expecting something like this then you are just fooling yourself. It is better to be a little disappointed, but it is important to be practical and realistic in such matters.

If you have the right approach, you will automatically take the right steps. Don't put too much pressure on yourself to start earning from the very beginning. It is important to give yourself some time to make some errors. This will help you to learn better. If you don't experiment, you will not grow. So, be easy on yourself while you do all that you can do for your vlog.

While it is important to be relaxed and easy, it is also important to be informed. How will you earn? Who will pay you? You need to understand these simple things. This chapter will help you in understanding the financial aspect related to vlogging. This will help you to plan your finances well. It will also help you to keep realistic goals for yourself in terms of finances and earnings.

**1. Subscribers and email marketing**

When you create a YouTube channel for yourself, there will be people who will decide to follow your channel and all the updates related to it. These people are your subscribers. These subscribers are the first ones to know when you upload a new vlog video on your channel.

After this, they have a choice to watch or skip the video. But, at least the word is out and they know that you have a new video on your vlog channel.

If you look at the most popular channels, you will notice that they have a large number of subscribers. If your subscribers are increasing each day, it only means you are becoming more and more popular.

Each vlogger aims at getting more and more subscribers. The higher the number of subscribers, the higher the number of views for your videos and also the amount of money that you earn. It is important that you understand as to how your subscribers will help you to earn money.

While the number of subscribers is definitely a way to assess the popularity of the vlog, it does not directly help you to earn money. As and when your subscribers increase, YouTube sets certain rewards for you. There are many small rewards when you reach a certain number of subscribers.

But, people who are serious about their vlogging aim for the big rewards. They work hard to achieve those greater rewards. YouTube will reward you with a silver play button if you are able to reach 100,000 subscribers. YouTube will reward you with a gold play button if you are able to reach 1,000,000 subscribers. YouTube will reward you with a diamond play button if you are able to reach 10,000,000 subscribers.

While the number of subscribers does not directly help you to earn money, it does have an indirect effect on the same. In fact, it has the most influential effect on your revenues. If you have a large number of subscribers, there is a greater chance that you will earn good revenues from YouTube. You should always aim to get more and more subscribers just like the popular vloggers on the Internet.

Subscribers, as mentioned, means people who have clicked the "follow" button and want to be informed each time you upload a new video. This is good sign as this clearly means people like what you are doing and want to see more. However, subscribers in the Interworld also means people who have "opted-in" on your email list via an opt-in box. This means, that, with a click of a button, you can send your subscriber and email with Auto Responder Software. A more detailed explanation follows.

### What is an opt-in box?
An opt-in box is another way of saying "somewhere for your visitors to enter their email address to receive updates and emails from you". Once a visitor has given you their email address, they have "opted-in". An opt-in box normally resembles the layout of the examples below:

## Back Pain Newsletter Sign Up

Receive Spine-health's FREE weekly back pain eNewsletter

Enter Email Address

☐ YES - send me special offers from health-friendly sponsors at Spine-health

SUBMIT

### Wikipedia definitions:

*Opt in email is a term used when someone is given the option to receive "bulk" email, that is, email that is sent to many people at the same time. Typically, this is some sort of mailing list, newsletter, or advertising. Obtaining permission before sending e-mail is critical because without it, the email is Unsolicited Bulk Email, better known as spam.*

*There are several common forms of opt-in email:*

### Unconfirmed opt-in

*A new subscriber first gives his or her email address to the list software (for instance, on a web page), but no steps are taken to make sure that this address actually belongs to the person. This can cause email from the mailing list to be considered spam because simple typos of the email address can cause the email to be sent to someone else. Malicious subscriptions are also possible, as are subscriptions that are due to spammers forging email addresses that are sent to the email address used to subscribe to the mailing list.*

## Confirmed opt-in (COI) or double opt-in

*A new subscriber asks to be subscribed to the mailing list, but unlike unconfirmed opt-in, a confirmation email is sent to verify it was really them. Many believe the person must not be added to the mailing list unless an explicit step is taken, such as clicking a special web link or sending back a reply email. This ensures that no person can subscribe someone else out of malice or error. Mail system administrators and non-spam mailing list operators refer to this as confirmed subscription or closed-loop opt-in.*

*Some marketers call closed loop opt-in "double opt-in."*

*The term double opt-in was coined by marketers in the late '90s to differentiate it from single opt-in, where a new subscriber to an email list gets a confirmation email telling them they will begin to receive emails if they take no action. This is compared to double opt-in, where the new subscriber must respond to the confirmation email to be added to the list.*

*Some marketers contend that double opt-in is like asking for permission twice and that it constitutes unnecessary interference with someone who has already said they want to hear from the marketer.*

*The term double opt-in has also been co-opted by spammers, diluting its value.*

## Opt-out

*Instead of giving people the option to be put on the list, they are automatically added and have the option to be taken out.*

### *End of Wikipedia definitions*

Here is an example of how a confirmation request email can look like after somebody opted-in to receive a newsletter :

As a vlogger you should always try to get double opt-ins by sending your opt-ins a confirmation email – see the above screenshot. Your opt-ins are then telling you twice that they want the information: first when they opted-in and a second time when they receive the confirmation email and click the confirmation link.

The double opt-ins are better as the chances of the emails ending up in your visitor's spam box are smaller. However in my experience a heck of a lot of emails (that I signed up for with double opt-in) end up in my spam box anyway.

This is called building a list. You have a list of 100.000 people if 100.000 people have opted-in. With the people on your list, you are going to use email marketing.

### What is email marketing?
Email marketing is one of the best ways - if done correctly - to keep existing visitors coming back and to market your offers directly to their inboxes. All you need to do is send the people who opt-in an email on a regular basis with links that will earn you money (affiliate marketing links, which is explained further in this book). The people that will receive your emails have given their permission, so it is permission-based email marketing and for this reason is not categorized as spam.

To sell a product, you sell yourself first. People have to like the sales person that is sitting on the other side of the customers' desk, otherwise the customer will not order. This is the same here: with email marketing you have a change to build a relationship with your customers. Give them good content, or interesting freebies and they will start to like you, giving you a better chance of selling to them. Lead generation is huge on the internet.

### *What is an auto responder?*

An auto responder is a software program that automatically sends out emails on a pre-scheduled basis to all opted-in people on your list.

Once you have built a list, the idea is that you send them some freebies or send them a newsletter or an affiliate link etc… You can't possibly do all this manually each time you receive a new opt-in. An autoresponder does this automatically for you. Let's say you want to create a 5 part email course. You set the intervals for the emails, say once a day. All you need to do is type in the emails once in your auto responder software and your list will get an email once a day. Anyone joining your list will automatically be sent those emails for the next 5 days. Important: you need to "build a relation ship" with your subscribers by sending them "normal" emails without any affiliate links. To give an example: if you are a beauty vlogger, you send several email about how well a certain product worked and you could ask your subscribers for feedback and to email you what they think about the product. In another email, you can tell your subscribers that you found a really cool, new product and tell them: "You can buy the product here". You will then link the here to your affiliate link so you will earn money when one of your subscribers buys a product through your affiliate link.

You must have an auto responder when you have an opt-in box on your website.

You will have seen these messages at the bottom of your emails :

To unsubscribe or change subscriber options visit:
http://www.aweber.com/z/r/?jAx.....

When you click on that click you will be unsubscribed. By law you need to put an unsubscribe button at the bottom of each email you send. If people no longer want to receive your emails and click unsubscribe, your auto responder will remove that person automatically from your list and your next pre-scheduled email will no longer be received by the person who has unsubscribed.

### *Which auto responder is best?*

The best email auto-responder on the market, is in my opinion www.aweber.com, but a good, free alternative is MailChimp (if using a limited list).

Here's a list of automated email auto responders:

www.aweber.com RECOMMENDED

www.getresponse.com
www.mailchimp.com

You have to make sure that you use a professional auto responder service because that way you are protected from spam complaints. If you can provide proof of subscriber opt-in you are in a strong position.

Note that most very good auto responders have a monthly fee. Often, the monthly fee increases the more subscribers you have.

### *What is affiliate marketing?*
In the "old days" a guy from the insurance company would come and sit in your kitchen and try to sell you insurance. The "older" generation reading this will remember. When he sold you some, his boss – the insurance company – would pay the sales guy say, 10% commission. That is affiliate marketing the old fashioned way. I guess you could also call it commission marketing because that's what it is: somebody gets paid commission for selling somebody else's product. The insurance company is the affiliate merchant, or vendor, and the sales guy is the affiliate as he gets commission from a sale.

Now imagine this scenario on the internet: the insurance company has a website that sells insurance. The sales guy has a website that tells you the pros and cons of insurance and here and there on his website he puts a link that, when you click on it, you have the chance to buy something. If you buy via that link, the insurance company will pay the sales guy commission.

So in this case you are the sales guy that will be selling for other companies, and every time you sell something, the company will pay you commission. You are the affiliate (the one who receives the commission) and the insurance company that will pay you is called the merchant or the vendor. All you need to do is put the same affiliate links on your website that refer to the insurance companies' website, and you get paid when somebody buys via that link. Where and how to get your money making affiliate link will be covered later in the book. Everything else is automated. Commissions range from 1% to 75%. Physical products usually pay between 2% and 25% commission but www.Clickbank.com, which sells mostly digital products, can pay up to 80% commission or even more.

*A merchant* is an online retailer with a website where you can buy products or services.

*An affiliate* or online publisher is the person who drives visitors to the merchant's website and gets paid commission when customers buy

78

something by clicking on the link that is on the affiliate's website. An affiliate drives buyers to the merchant's sites and gets paid for it. The merchants pays the affiliate commission only when a sale is made. The affiliate will sell your product or services for a commission. Affiliates are other internet marketers or other website owners.

www.amazon.com is a good example of a successful affiliate merchant business, which it started in 1996. They now have over 400,000 affiliates (Amazon calls them associates). A vendor is the person who is selling his goods on Amazon and Amazon gets paid commission (or a vendor's fee) every time the vendor sells something. The vendor of course gets the money for the purchase of the goods (minus Amazon's commission). All administration and collecting of the money is done by Amazon.

www.amazon.com and www.comparethemarket.com are probably two companies that you have heard of before but never realised that they made money in affiliate marketing.

Amazon is a merchant as you can sell their products as an affiliate but in a way Amazon is also an affiliate network as all administration is done by them.

Affiliate marketing is literally everywhere on the web. Websites without any money-making links are hard to find these days.

*Affiliate networks* are automated websites on which merchants can put their name to say they are looking for affiliates to drive traffic to their websites. You, as an affiliate, go to the affiliate network to grab an affiliate link to put on your website. The affiliate network pays you your commission. All you need to do is stick a link on your site and drive traffic, all the rest is done automatically for you. I will give some examples of trustworthy networks later in this book.

*Affiliate marketing* is the whole automated set up to do with affiliates, merchants and affiliate networks.

So, back to list building and your email subscribers. You will become "an affiliate" and sell products (with your affiliate link) to your subscribers. You can put your affiliate link in emails, on your videos, on your website, etc..

**Being an affiliate has the following advantages:**

- No licence fees needed

- There is no contract to sign with anybody

- You can log onto your work anywhere in the world

- You can make money while you sleep ( after you have put in some hard work)

- You can sell in any country, worldwide

- You can sell in any niche

- You never have to process orders

- You never ever have to ship orders

- You never ever need to worry about stock take, over stock or left over stock

- You never need a customers' service email or telephone number

- You never need large start-up capital to begin trading

- You never need a Payment Processing Gateway ( a bank that charges your customer's card)

- You don't need employees

- You don't need sales experience

- You don't need to know anything about the niche to sell in it

- You have no production costs to worry about

- You never have to leave your house

- You never have to speak to anybody if you don't want to

- You can choose the hours you work

- You can be your own boss

- You can start up a business that can grow 200% or more each year, which is almost impossible to achieve in a business outside the web

- You never have to go to the bank to pay in cheques, as all is done electronically

- You never have to chase late payments as all is paid in advance

- There are no cash flow problems (if you manage your money correctly) as you receive your money immediately

### *URL-shortening software or link-cloaking software*

URL stands for: Unique Rescource Locator and is just another name for a website, the website you see on top of your browser, in the top bar. Sometimes an affiliate link is so long and looks so unattractive that you might want to shorten it before sending it to potential customers. That's what URL-shortening means. You can get from this URL:
www.amazon.co.uk/Head-Ti-S6-Titanium-Tennis-Racket/dp/B001DMKZSQ/ref=sr_1_2?s=sports&ie=UTF8&qid=1294687755&sr

To this URL:
www.tennis-racket/Tintanium When people click on this they will be re-directed to the Amazon website as shown above with your affiliate link.

Here are two URL-shortening websites:
www.bitly.com
www.tiny.cc
www.tinyurl.com
www.goo.gl

For more, just search for them. Make sure that you read the terms and conditions as some of these websites will automatically delete your URL if it's not used or clicked on for a certain number of days.

### 2. Number of views

The one thing that directly helps you to earn money from vlogging is the number of views your video gets. Each video will have a count of the number of views that the video has had. The more the number of people who view your videos the better your revenue will be from the views.

It should be noted here that a person clicking on your video link does not need to view the entire video to lock it as a view. A 30 second view is considered as a view on YouTube. But, it is always better that the viewer watches more than that because it means that they are enjoying your work or at least giving you a chance. There is a chance that they will view your other videos too.

It is a little more complex than just the number of views on the video. The country you belong to also affects the amount of money you earn from

YouTube. YouTube gives no official confirmation on how much a newbie vlogger will earn.

According to the available statistics, you can earn one dollar for a thousand views. This means that if you are aiming to earn 1000 dollars, you need at least a million views on a particular video of yours. Some vloggers have also reported that it is possible to earn five dollars for one thousand views. But, no matter how much you earn, there is a percentage that YouTube will take from you. It is providing you a platform to represent yourself, while earning money, so it is justified.

YouTube will get forty five per cent of what you will earn from your videos. There are many factors that influence the amount of money you will be making from YouTube videos. The first and foremost thing is the number of views that you are able to garner. But, that is not the only thing.

YouTube is interested in knowing how engaged a viewer is in your videos. This will affect your revenue. You can only calculate a rough estimate of your future earnings in the beginning. You will only know something for sure as and when you go along. The advertisements that your videos broadcast will also affect your revenue.

It should be noted that you can earn from a video even a year after it was made. As and when you get views and you hit the desired mark, you will start earning. This again proves that content is the king. In the beginning, nobody will know you. You will only have handful of subscribers who will be your friends, family and acquaintances. But, this is no excuse to make low quality content.

Always look at the larger picture. A year from now, your subscribers will increase. More often than not, these people will start digging out the older videos that you made. Before you know, the older videos that you would have made will be all over the Internet. This is where your content will help you.

You might not immediately earn from it, but with time, the good work that you do will pay off and that too in a big way. So, this is like a chain. The better content you have, the more number of subscribers you will have. More the number of subscribers you have, there are better chances to have good number of views for your videos.

## 3. Advertisements

Another, and a very important, way to earn money from your YouTube channel is through advertisements. You can earn through Google's

Adsense (you will have to create an account with Google) and through direct brand deals that you will be making as a vlogger. Various brands selling all kinds items understand the importance of vlogging in today's world. They understand that there might be not be many people watching the television, but everybody is on the Internet.

Long ago, newspapers, billboards and television advertisements were the only means for brands to promote their products. But today, things are different. Internet is everywhere. It is only getting bigger and bigger.

A kid, a teenager, an adult, just about everybody is hooked on to the Internet. This is what the brands want to exploit now. They understand that vloggers have a certain reach. They are followed and the more popular ones are almost worshipped like stars. If the brand can utilize the vloggers' strengths to its own favour, it is great for the brand. They pay the vlogger they work with.

The vlogger earns money and the brand gets to promote their product. You might be worried about how you can tap in to this world and how much you can tap in to, but you need not worry. A subsequent chapter explains in detail what needs to be done to contact various brands.

It should be noted that you are not on your own here. There is a body above you that governs how this all works. This will also be explained in detail in the subsequent chapter. For now, you need to know that you should be honest with your viewers.

If you are advertising a product, you need to make it very clear in your content that it is an advertisement. The viewer should know that he is watching an advertisement and the vloggers are getting paid for it. Of course, how much you get paid stays with YouTube, you and the brand. But, the viewer should not be fooled into believing that the advertisement is a part of the content. This will be against the law.

While you are worrying about how much you will make from advertisements, you need to know that it will directly depend on your popularity as a vlogger and also the brand status. A big brand pays better than a smaller one. But, then a bigger brand will only associate itself with vloggers who are really popular and have many subscribers.

You should remember that a brand will never invest in you if they don't see a benefit and gain. Just because you are vlogger, you will not get paid. It again comes to the quality of your vlog. The better your content, the more popular you'll get. It is as simple as that.

You can also earn money from Banner Advertising. This means that companies or individuals will pay you a fee so their banner will be shown on your website. This is great income as it will create a monthly income stream for you as mostly this type of advertising is a fixed monthly fee.

## 4. Your website

It is very important to use a good hosting company for your website otherwise, when you become a well-known vlogger and your website will have LOTS of visitors, it will become too slow to make it a pleasurable experience for your visitors on your website. A website with a lot of videos also needs some time to load so choosing your hosting company and the right bandwidth is very important.

### *What is 'hosting'?*
Once you have decided on your domain name, which is the name of your site, such as www.yourdomainnamehere.com you need to make sure that somebody will host your website. This means somebody has got to store your website somewhere so people can access it. When you have built a website on your computer and it has been published to the web, people need to be able to see it. If 1000 people want to look at your site, they won't come to your home or office to do it, so you need to have a place where your site is "hosted" so that all 1000 people can look at it at the same time. This is what a hosting company does; they will give your site a space on their massive computer servers so people can view it. You pay the hosting company a fee to host, or store, your site.

When choosing a hosting company, you need to look at two factors: web disk space and bandwidth, both explained in the next few paragraphs.

Another reason why you need a hosting company is because of the bandwidth (see explanation below) on your computer. If you host your website yourself and have an internet connection speed of 1MB on your home computer, it will take several hours for a customer to download a movie. A hosting company might have a 250MB internet connection speed, meaning your customers can download the movie much quicker.

Choose your hosting company carefully. You can spend a heck of a lot of time designing your site but if it is slow to load due to a poor hosting plan, visitors will move on to another site. I recommend strongly not using the free or very cheap web hosting companies.

**- What is bandwidth and what is the difference with web disk space?**
This often confuses IM newbies.

## What is 'disk space'?

Disk space is also called data storage or hosting space. It is the amount of data that the hosting provider allows you to store. Images, audio files, visual files, multi-media files and graphics all take up a lot more space than simple text. If your site has 20 pages of mostly text, your total disk space needs will probably be under 1MB. If you have a site with lots of graphics and multimedia, you need a lot more disk space.

> **Top Tip: To find out how much disk space you need for your website, simply put all your website files into one folder on your PC. Right click the folder and choose 'properties', which will show you the total space needed to store your website.**

## What is 'bandwidth'?

Bandwidth is the amount of traffic that your hosting company allows between your website on their server, and the visitors to your website. It is a measure of total data transferred in one month to and from your site. Each time a visitor looks at your site, it is downloaded from your hosting company to be viewed on the internet. If you go over the amount of bandwidth with your hosting company they could charge you an extra fee, visitors might not be able to see your site or it will be downloaded very slowly.

Think about bandwidth as cars on motorways (highways in the US). If you are the only car on the motorway, you can drive quickly but the more cars the slower you're forced to go. You are also not able to overtake another car when you are stuck in a queue. With low bandwith your visitors cannot download things quickly and will be stuck in a queue when wanting to download a file if two people want to download it at the same time.

## How much bandwidth do you need?

For most small businesses or personal sites 2GB of bandwidth per month is usually enough. Most hosting companies will include this in their cheapest package. Traffic to your site is the number of 'bits' that are transferred on the internet. One gigabyte (GB) is 1,024 megabytes. To store one character, one byte of storage is needed.

- Imagine that you have 100 filing cabinets in your office.

- Each of these filing cabinets has 1000 folders in it

- In each folder there are 100 papers

- On each paper are 100 characters

85

- The total of all these is 1 GB (100x1000x100x100)

How much bandwidth you need depends on what type of website you are building. For videos, a lot of bandwidth is needed. If people can download MP3 songs or movies from your website, and you are expecting a lot of visitors, you will need a very high bandwidth because each MP3 song is, on average, about 4MB. A movie can be up to 1000MB or 1GB. In this case, if you only have a bandwidth of 1GB, when two customers want to download a 1GB movie, they cannot do it at the same time. Remember, in my comparison with motorways and cars you cannot overtake a car when in a traffic jam. The second one in the queue will probably receive an error message. This will result in your customer having a negative impression of your site, which of course you must avoid. If you are expecting ten thousand visitors to your site per day, you need to choose the correct bandwidth plan with your hosting company. Most hosting companies offer the facility to start with low bandwidth and upgrade it at an extra cost.

Companies offer a variety of bandwidth options in terms of your monthly gigabyte allocation.

Work out how much bandwidth you need is not as simple as calculating how much disk space you need. But the following formula will give you some idea: Size (or disk space) of all your web pages including all graphics X numbers of visitors you expect each day X number of pages your visitors will view X 30 days per month = total monthly data transfer, or bandwidth.

The amount of emails that you send also counts in the bandwidth. If you often send hundreds of emails with very large files attached, it will count towards your bandwidth usage.

If your website gets lots of visits per month, through Google or from affiliates sending traffic to it, you need more bandwidth, not necessarily more space.

Quite a few hosting companies now offer unlimited bandwidth. More and more hosting companies start to offer unlimited space and unlimited bandwidth.

**Conclusion:** disk space is the amount of storage space your website needs on the server of your hosting company. Bandwidth is the traffic that passes through your hosting company to your website.

Unfortunately, you will have a monthly fee to pay for your hosting. Once you will have millions of people visiting your site, the hosting fee could cost a few hundred dollars per month, at least.

You can buy a domain name from one company and have the hosting done by another company. Personally I prefer to use the company I bought my domain from to do the hosting as well.

If you have an Australian website and you are targeting a market in Australia, it is always best to choose a hosting company with an Australian server. If you are based in USA, choose a hosting company with a USA based server and so on. This can be important for search engine ranking purposes.

I've always used GoDaddy (www.godaddy.com) and 1and1 (www.1and1.com) for my hosting. If you're still looking for a hosting provider then I recommend www.godaddy.com, especially if you make mostly Wordpress-based websites.

Generally I prefer www.1and1.com because I like their platform better than GoDaddy's and in my experience they have better customer services, which you can contact late during weekdays and also on weekends. Each time I have phoned 1and1 with a problem, I had an immediate answer, but I cannot say the same for GoDaddy.

Another advantage of www.1and1.com is that you can have almost unlimited free emails for each domain name, if you choose the business option. With GoDaddy you only get *one* email account but you can purchase more.

However, for Wordpress sites, I have come across some problems with www.1and1.com and therefore www.godaddy.com is recommended if you are planning to use Wordpress.

Here some other reliable hosting companies:

www.hostgator.com

www.hostmonster.com

www.justhost.com

## 5. Put affiliate links on your website

You can put content and affiliate links on your website. To find affiliate products that you can sell, search for your keyword + affiliates. If you vist a site and scroll to the bottom, there is often text visible like this: earn money with us, affiliates, associates, etc.... Click on those links and sign up with those affiliate networks. When somebody buys something though your affiliate link, you've earned money.

## 6. Merchandise

Depending on what kind of vlog you have, you can offer merchandise to your followers. If you search for "short run printing of T-shirts" for instance you will find plenty of companies that can deliver a small quantity with any printing you require to be on the T-shirt. You could also offer mugs, memory sticks, mousemats, bags, etc…

Offering merchandise can work particularly well if a charity is involved in your vlog.

## 7. Books

You might be a vlogger on certain health issues. So, why not publish/sell a book about it! You don't have to be a writer to write a book! These days, you can let somebody else write your book; the person who will write the book is called a ghost writer. You pay the writer a fee and all the copyrights of the books are yours, therefore you will be paid the royalties. You will "outsource" the writing of the book. Outsourcing is simply giving a task to somebody, and paying them to do it. Outsourcing on the Internet is done on outsourcing websites. Almost anything can be outsourced on the Internet.

If you search for "outsourcing websites", you will find a lot of website where people are waiting to do jobs for you. I can recommend www.upwork.com to find writers for your book.

Talking about outsourcing: www.fiverr.com is another great side to get jobs done but this site is more for "smaller" jobs and less suitable to find a ghost writer.

Once your book is written, all you need is a cover (somebody on Fiverr can do this for you) and you can self-publish your book, which is totally free on some website e.g. www.kdp.amazon.com = Amazon's Kindle Publishing Platform and www.createspace.com to publish a printed book.

## 8. How soon will you start earning money?

It is important that you understand that it is very difficult to earn good money from vlogging in the beginning. This is because nobody knows you. Why would they watch your videos? It is only with time, they will start noticing you.

And, if you are doing good work, then it will slowly get easier for you. The best bet you can have is to keep making good quality video content frequently. The more people notice you, the better your chances become.

You should also understand that it is much more difficult today to earn money than it was 4-5 years ago. When vlogging came into being, there were very few vloggers. Most people did not know what vlogging was. Even the ones who knew about it didn't know that you could earn money from it. This made it easier for vloggers of those times.

Things were very different then. They have changed a lot, and rapidly, since then. Now, there are so many vloggers. If you go on the Internet, you will be shocked to see the number of videos. This makes it difficult for all. But, it is important to understand that though things are more difficult, if you are serious about this and have enough passion, you can get into the top bracket sooner or later.

Though the number of vloggers has increased, the number of audiences has also increased. This means there is more scope for different kinds of content. There is no one content that is ruling.

Everybody has good Internet speed now, so the viewer base has increased at a rapid speed. This changes the entire dynamic. The competition has increased, but the opportunities have also increased.

In the beginning, you need to focus on the basic things, such as promoting on Facebook and twitter and coming out with a video regularly. The other things will only follow. It is only a matter of time. You should always remember that good content and right marketing is the way to go. If you are sorted in these two departments then you have a higher chance of making it big.

However, it is highly advised to not expect a million views and millions of bucks in your pocket from your first videos. That is unrealistic. If you are in college, start vlogging as a side thing. Slowly as you understand more of it and how it is working for you, devote yourself more to it.

If you are in a job, then don't just quit because your friend makes good money out of the vlog. You will be disappointed to see the result in the beginning.

If you are not able to handle pressure and disappointment in the beginning, it will not get better for you. Don't quit that job unless you are sure that this works for you, irrespective of whether it has worked for your friend or not. Try to be sorted on your finances in the beginning so that there is no pressure on you in the beginning.

It would be nothing but crazy if you are expecting your vlog to take care of all your finances right from the beginning. This is nothing but a recipe for disappointment. You have to take it easy for the first few months if you want this to work for you.

Once you are all set up, ready to send traffic to your site, how soon you will start earning money all depends on how soon you will get thousands of visitors.

### *What is traffic?*
Getting traffic to your site simply means getting people to see your site. It is no good having a site if nobody can find it. To put it very simply: *traffic = visitors = people looking at your site.* Always use different traffic techniques because not everybody uses the same method of finding products on the web. If you are selling a product outside the Internet you would use different methods to try to find customers. You can go to exhibitions, you can sell at markets, you can call people and make appointments and you can place advertisements in magazine and newspapers. If you're selling products on a market, the more you visit the more you sell because different people in different areas go to different markets. Exactly the same happens online: different types of people will search for your products; from different religions, different traditions, different intellectual levels and different backgrounds. Everybody has different knowledge and people use their own knowledge to search for products. If you only focus on getting traffic with Facebook, you are missing out on all the people that do not use Facebook.

Here are a few ways to send traffic to your site. If you think you might use one of these traffic methods, please Google for more information as each method is different and beyond the scope of this book to go into detail for each method.

- Article marketing

- Forum posting

- Interviews

- offering freebies on your website

- Podcasting

- Press release

- Putting an op-tin box on your site

- Radio

- SEO

- Social networks

- Video marketing

- Webinars

There are also several paid traffic methods, to name but a few:

- Banner Advertising

- CPV (Clicks Per View) marketing

- Facebook ads and other social media ads

- Magazine ads

- Mobile Phone Marketing

- Online ads

- PPC (Pay Per Click advertising)

- Solo Ads

- Sponsored reviews

- Youtube ads

# Chapter 8: Marketing

After you have made your videos and edited them well, the next obvious step is to market them. Nobody will come to your home to watch the videos. Even after you have posted them online, you will have to take steps to market the videos well. This is important because people have to know about the video to watch it.

If they don't know that any such video exists, how will they watch it? Once more and more people watch the video and like it, it will get easier. But, in the beginning you will have to take dedicated steps to do the marketing well.

Marketing, these days, is a necessary evil. Whether you like it or not, you can't escape it. If you look around, marketing for various things is happening all around us at all the times. Somebody is selling soap and shampoo through a television advertisement. Somebody is marketing something on the radio. There are people who are selling and marketing door to door. Marketing is happening all around us and at all times.

When you wish to be a successful vlogger, you actually wish to be many things at the same time. It means to be a good researcher, a good director, a script writer, a good producer, a good cameraman, a good editor and good marketing personnel.

You have to combine all these skills to be a good vlogger. If you follow your favourite vloggers, you will see that all of them have to make efforts to market what they have shot. When you market your video, you make an attempt to make it visible to as many people as possible. The greater the number of people who watch your videos, the better it is for you.

Amateur vloggers get so consumed by the entire process of researching and filming the video that they very easily forget this very important aspect of vlogging. They often fail to market their videos well.

This means that not many people end up watching their videos. This can be very heart breaking for an amateur. If you don't pay attention to such things in the very beginning, you will only end up losing your confidence and giving up.

To save yourself from falling into this trap of less confidence and constant failing, learn to adapt and adopt skills that are useful for you in the long run.

You can follow the following simple steps to make sure that you are marketing your vlog well:

## 1. Connecting to other social medias

Once you have made your video, you will definitely post on your YouTube account. YouTube allows you to connect it to other social media accounts that you might have. This can be very useful because it will help you to make your video more visible.

First and foremost, make sure that you have accounts of other social media platforms. You need to be as active as possible on these accounts.

### Facebook account

www.facebook.com As a vlogger, you should have a Facebook account. If you are one of those who believe that it is not necessary then you need to change. This platform will allow you to connect with people very easily. You don't have to call up people and tell them that you have a new video. Your news feed will automatically show that there is something new you have posted.

It is important that you make an effort to connect on Facebook. When people like your videos and say something good, remember to acknowledge them. They are taking out time for you. You need to be thankful. Even if someone doesn't like your video, don't be rude.

Accept the criticism positively. Be active on this platform and engage with people. You can also form a fan page. Facebook allows you to do that. This fan page could have links to all the videos that you have uploaded. Insist your online friends to join you on our fan page. You can run contests or post interesting stuff now and then to keep the page interesting for people.

### Twitter account

www.twitter.com You also need to have a twitter account. It will be great if you can keep the same name for channel name and the twitter handle name. This will make it easier for your audience to recognize you. You should be as active on twitter as on Facebook.

If you have good number of followers on twitter then this could mean that these people will follow you on your vlog and will invest their time to watch your video.

There is a chance that you are not very fond of marketing. You might consider it a shameless thing to do to ask people again and again to watch your videos. No matter how you feel, this is something that you have to do. You will have to make an effort to publicize because all your hard work is dependent on this.

If you don't tell people about your work, how would they know that you are a great content creator? Don't worry, you can hire a manager once you are popular. Till then, work hard on your marketing skills as much as on your vlogs. And, you don't have to ask people again and again. Just post a link, add a great tag line and invite people to watch. You can always publicize in a smart way.

Facebook and Twitter are generally known as the best social media sites to hang around. However, there are millions of people hanging around on other sites so make sure you are also present on at least some of the sites listed below.

- APP www.app.net

- BeMyEyes www.bemyeyes.com

- Devianart www.devianart.com

- Flickr www.flickr.com

- Google Plus www.plus.google.com

- Instagram www.instagram.com

- Linkedin www.linkedin.com

- MySpace www.myspace.com

- Pinterest www.pinterest.com

- Tagged www.tagged.com

- Tumblr www.tumblr.com

- Tumblr www.tumblr.com

- Vine www.vine.co

- VK www.vk.com

Check out online in which countries these social media sites are most popular, before you decide to use the sites.

## 2. Being creative

A simple mantra of marketing is to be creative. You can be creative in the way you introduce your videos or in the way you give them a title. For example, if you have a vlog on what you ate for the day, you can set a little story and make it fun for the audience. You could start the buzz a couple of days before really uploading the video.

You have to find ways that the audience find it hard to avoid you. Your creativity should force them to have a look at the video. Find out new and innovative ways each time to introduce your video. Ask people for suggestions on what they would like to watch on your video.

Keep people engaged and wanting for more. This is the way that you will grow and reach out to many more people. If a Facebook contact likes your video, he will share it on his Facebook page. His contact list will be able to see it on his page. They in turn will watch it and subscribe to your channel. Some of them will share it on their page. This chain reaction will help you to grow and increase your followers.

Once you have started uploading videos regularly, you will start understanding whether people are enjoying your vlog or not. You will get an idea if things are going right for you. Is the number of positive comments increasing? Are your subscribers increasing? Ask these simple questions to yourself every now and then. If the answer is no, you need to pep up things. You will have to study your vlog and marketing strategy and understand what is not working in your favour. You will surely find a way to improve.

You can get some t-shirts printed with your channel name. You can wear these t-shirts regularly in your videos. You can also start various contests and courier it to people who win. These are simple ways to make people know more about you your channel. It is also important that you are dressed well in all your videos.

You are marketing yourself all the time, so when you are untidy, you are sending a wrong message. You have to make people like you, your personality and your vlog. It is all linked together. People will come to your channel because they like your personality or your style of presentation or your speaking or your content or all of these factors. So, when you are thinking of marketing, you have to improve on all these aspects of vlogging also.

## 3. Being regular

It is important that you are regular with your videos. Even if people like you, they will forget you. There are so many vloggers out there. Nobody will sit and wait for you. Plan a calendar for yourself and make sure that you upload new content regularly. Once people start liking you, they will watch more and more of you. They will tell their friends about you. This is another way of marketing. Be consistent, and this will help you to grow.

When you are consistent, people will start connecting with you. They will look out for you. You will also notice that with time, you will get some ardent admirers. These followers will even start snubbing people who comment negatively for you. This is called growing a fan base.

You can only grow a fan base if you are regularly giving your fans what they want and expect from you. This is how you will form a relationship and a strong bond with them. So, make sure to be regular. Don't make your subscribers wait for days and weeks for a video.

When you start vlogging, you will see that you will get it all, love and hatred too. There will be people who will encourage your creativity and style and will motivate you to work harder. On the other hand, there would be people who would put you down and criticize you in the worst of ways. It can get very overwhelming for a new vlogger to handle this kind of pressure.

Many amateur vloggers find themselves struggling with pressure that dislikes and negative comments have on them. These amateurs take things very seriously at a personal level and are unable to deal with such things.

There are many people who are naturally inclined to handle stress in a better way. And, then there are many people who struggle with this. They don't know how to handle criticism and hatred. They find themselves getting too involved, which in turn reduces their productivity at work.

If you are one of those who know how to handle negative comments in a light hearted and positive manner, then you are better prepared for vlogging. But, if you are one of those who have no idea what to do when they read anything negative about their work, then you need to prepare yourself.

Every vlogger has to go through this phase. While some got through it in the early stages of their career, many others have to struggle throughout. If you have ten positive comments on your video today, there is no guarantee that it will be the same tomorrow. You could have ten negative comments tomorrow. This is the world of vlogging. You do your very best and then leave it for the audience to judge.

It is impossible to predict how people will react. Internet gives a lot of freedom to everybody. While you have the freedom to make videos and share your opinions in them, the people have the choice and the freedom to dislike or like them. Some people get a little over board and get negative. But, that again is not in your control.

The best thing that you can do in this scenario is to be better prepared in terms of handling the negativity. This will save your peace of mind, which is very essential when you are in a creative world. Don't be scared of negativity; instead just learn how to deal with it in the most positive of ways. If you learn to handle it well, your job is half done. In my opinion, the best way to handle negativity is not to handle it! Just ignore it. You can simply never please everybody. If you get 10 Dislikes, just focus on getting another 100 likes. Most people will pay attention to the Likes and ignore the Dislikes.

From a more technical point of view, you need to understand how the viewers can react to what they see in your vlog. Nobody is coming to your house or writing you letters to tell you what they think. There are two ways that enable the viewers and the audience to react and express what they feel about your work:

- Likes or dislikes
- Comments

**Likes or dislikes**

The viewers can like or dislike the video that you have put up. If they like it, then you should be happy because that is what you wanted. But, if they dislike it then you need to know how to handle this.

To begin with, it is not possible that everybody likes your video. No matter what video you go to on the internet, it will have a few likes and a few dislikes. This is very normal. It is important that you don't have any unreal expectations that every person liking the video will like it. People are different. They have different tastes and opinions in life. The people who like your video understand your point of view and people who don't like it don't understand it, which is fine.

The people who dislike your videos don't hate you. They just don't understand your opinions. You should remember to not take it personally. A smart person will understand the problem, find a solution and move on. Don't get too attached to such things if you want to be successful.

Now, the question is whether the likes are more than the dislikes and what is the ratio of the likes to the dislikes. This will help you to understand where you stand. This will also help you to know what needs to be done.

You should always remember to take nothing to heart. No matter how much hard work you have put into your vlog, there are always chances that things will turn upside down. You will always have people who will not like what you do. The idea is to take nothing personally. Even if somebody is criticizing you in a negative way, remind yourself to not get bothered. You can always work harder and improve your work.

Feedback is important for any artist. It helps you to get better. But, you should know the difference between constructive feedback and a negative comment. Positive feedback is aimed at helping you to get better. It tells you the areas that can be improved upon. The intention is to motivate you and help you to get better.

On the other hand, a negative comment is aimed at putting you down. The only intention in a negative comment is to show a person how bad he is and also make him believe that he can't get better. You should know the difference between the two. You have to learn to take negative feedback and learn from it.

You will also have to learn to ignore negative comments. You should not give too much importance to negative people. There are some people who waste their time and energy in fighting such negative comments. They get perturbed and lose their cool. If you want to make the most of your time, remember not to indulge in such things. Always keep your head high and work harder than ever.

While you are taking on the journey of vlogging, you need to be prepared to find all kinds of people. You should be mentally prepared to get all kinds of comments.

When you are mentally prepared, it makes it a little easier to deal with a problem when it shows up. You concentrate on the positive and shed away the negative if you wish to create a healthy work space for yourself.

## 4. YouTube alternatives

As a vlogger, your primary goal would be to post on YouTube. But, along with YouTube, there are video channels where you can upload your videos as not everybody watches YouTube videos. The advantage of these channels is that they have different monetization and copy right policies. So, you should post on them if they provide you with what you are looking for for your vlog. Make sure you always check the copy right policies for each site before you upload your videos.

- www.dailymotion.com: Daily motion is one of the most popular websites for posting and viewing videos. In appearance, it is quite similar to YouTube.

Daily motion allows a vlogger to sell a subscription to make money. You can also monetize your content to improve your revenue. Daily motion is considered to be for vloggers who are really serious about vlogging. If vlogging is more than a hobby for you and of you are looking for something more than fun, then daily motion is for you.

- https://vimeo.com: Vimeo is a good platform for various vloggers. The home page of this website has a list of videos that have been personally selected by the staff for their innovation and creativity.

You can also post short films on this website. There some great videos by some exceptional short film makers posted on this website. There is lesser number of advertisements on this website as compared to YouTube.

This platform is especially good for amateur vlogging. The budding vloggers get constructive criticism rather than negative feedback. Good quality vlogs on this channel will help you to learn and grow as a vlogger. This could help you in the long run.

You will have access to better privacy controls on this website. You can decide who all can view your videos. Basically, the aim is to give the creator maximum control over his content.

Here are a few more alternatives to Youtube (some are payable):

- Blip.tv - http://www.makerstudios.com/

- Brightcove – www.brightcove.com

- Buzznet – www.buzznet.com

- Daily Motion - www.dailymotion.com

- Dropshots  – www.dropshots.com

- Fark  – www.fark.com/video

- Flickr Video - https://www.flickr.com/search/?text=video&media=videos

- Metacafe - http://www.metacafe.com/

- Revver - http://www.mefeedia.com/site/revver

- Senuke - www.senuke.com

- The Open Video Project - https://open-video.org/

- Twitch - https://www.twitch.tv/

- Ustream - www.ustream.tv

- Viddler - www.viddler.com

- Videojug - http://www.videojug.com/

- Wittyfeed - https://www.wittyfeed.com/

# Chapter 9: Growing your Channel

Once you have followed all of the above steps and created your channel, found your theme and decided on some content for your vlogs, you need to grow your channel in order to start making money. Search engines favour video over written content as it is more profitable, because it holds audiences longer, so it is important that your videos stand out in search engines. In this chapter I will list some top tips to help you grow your YouTube channel.

**Great Titles**

- Keep the titles short and to the point, with less than 10 words in the title (under 100 characters)
- Use numbers if you can to optimise search engine turnout
- Add the most important keywords to the title e.g. if it is a makeup tutorial, make sure to add in 'makeup tutorial'.

**Vlog Description**

- Make sure keywords are also in your decription. There are a lot of characters available in the description, and you want to use them all! Make sure to use as many keywords as you can, but make sure the description is coherent and makes sense!
- First 160 characters will act as the google search metadescription, so make sure your keywords are included in these first characters.
- Add your first link right after the first 160 characters. YouTube will be suspicious if you put your link in these 160 characters.
- Always add more information about yourself, website, services etc.
- Finish decriptions with links to ALL of your other services and social media networks e.g. Twitter, Facebook, your blog etc.

**Tagging**

- Create tags about what people type into the search field. YouTube allows 500 characters for the tag section- make sure to use all of them! E.g. makeup tutorial for pale skin, how to do your makeup etc.
- Describe your videos with single words in the single word tags, e.g. makeup, tutorial, website, blog etc.

- Include at least one unique tag that is common to all of your videos. E.g. YourBrand1345. This will increase the chances that all of the 'next- up' videos will be your videos!

## Video Thumbnail

- Include text! As your video is shared, it won't include the title, so you want your thumbnail to include the title so that people will still click on the video to learn more
- Make sure that the vlog content is accurately portrayed in the text
- Use bright colours to get the audiences' attention
- Be consistent. This will help you to develop a brand.

## Audience Retention

- This is how long people spend watching your videos. The longer someone watches the video, the better your ranking on YouTube!
- One psychological trigger is called 'opening the loop'. This encourages the viewer to finish the video. Leave the audience hanging so they have to wait to the end for the big reveal.

## 'Call to Action'

- At the end of the video, ALWAYS ask the viewer to take the action of liking the video, subcribing to you or sharing the video. The viewer has taken the time to watch your video, and often the viewer wants to like, comment and subcribe, but they just need a prompt.
- This is a measure of engagement for YouTube, which will also help you in YouTube ranking.
- You can also ask the viewer multiple times, such as, 'if you like this lipstick leave a comment'.

## Subtitles/ Closed Caption

- Make sure subtitles are on. So many people requested this feature that YouTube spent millions creating it. It is also a big factor in your ranking on YouTube. YouTube will favour vidoes with Closed Caption videos (subtitles).
- You can use YouTube's own software to create the Closed Captions.

## Making Money

- Industry experts believe that YouTube ranks your video higher if you use YouTube/ Google AdSense.

- People have come to expect that they are going to watch ads, so people are not offended by this, so don't be afraid of it.
- Go to www.youtube.com/account_monetization and this will give you more information.

**First week of your video**

- The first week of your vlog is very important. YouTube will focus its traffic efforts to your vlog in the first week to test engagement, comments, likes etc.
- The first week of your video being live, make sure you share the video all over the Internet, send to friends, family, post it on blogs etc.
- The more people that see your video in the beginning, the higher your video will be ranked on YouTube.

# Chapter 10: Talent managers

Once you have understood how to make videos, the next challenge you will face is to market them well. There will be times when even after doing it all, you will not be able to increase the visibility of your vlogs. There are some vloggers who just give up at this stage. There are many others who decide to take professional help for their vlogging business.

It is important that you get good revenue from your vlogging; otherwise you will lose interest very soon. The professionals that can help you with your vlogging career are the talent managers. There are many talent management companies these days. These companies have helped many vloggers to reach great heights and they continue to help them even now. You will be learning about many such talent management companies in this chapter.

The talent management companies that help the vloggers to increase their revenue are called Multi Channel Network or MCN. There are some MCNs that are ruling the business. Some of them are Gleam Futures and Mode Media. The talent agency is a media consultancy that helps you to reach out to more and more people. They help you to manage your business well. You start out your vlog at a very small level, but as and when you do well, it becomes a fully-fledged business.

You need a manager to manage the ever-increasing business. If you do well, the talent management agency also gains recognition. They also expand and get more and more clients. So, while you are in this for your gain, they are in this for their gain. And, in the process, you will help each other.

## 1. What do you need a talent manager for?

A talent manager can help you fix the various issues that you could be facing in your vlogging business. They could help you to collaborate with other youtubers or could help you to optimize your content. You should be clear about what you are looking for. A talent manager could typically help you with the following:

- Are you strolling with the limited number of subscribers on your YouTube channel? Do you want to collaborate with some big players of the game but have no idea how to go about this? The MCN can help you with this.

- You have learnt all that you could about vlogging and youtube channels. But, you are still struggling with optimisation of content on your videos. Do you need some professional advice for the same? The talent manager will be the one to give you some professional advice.

- Every vlogger has the ultimate dream to increase the number of views on his vlogs. But, sometimes you could find yourself in a deadlock. You wouldn't know how to move forward after a certain point. Maybe, you have come a long way, but there seems no way from here. If you are at such a deadlock, then the MCN can be your professional help.

- Do you wish to get better revenue from your video ads? The talent manager can look into the reasons for your limited revenue and can help you with this.

- If you are looking at leveraging your channel to attract more clients and customers then the talent manager could have a solution for you.

A talent manager will help you deal with other aspects of the business, while you are busy working on your content. You should remember that the day you stop producing good content, you will lose it all. Your followers and subscribers might give you a couple of chances, but that's it.

At no stage in your vlogging career can you sit and think that I have done it all. I can take it easy now. You have to work like a machine that keeps delivering. This is the only way. You should never forget why all the subscribers signed onto your channel and why you have the brands working with you that are working with you.

It is for the entertainment and content that you provide them. So, make sure you keep doing that. But, there is another catch here. Earlier in your career, you will have more time. If all goes well for you and your channel becomes a hit, you'll only get busier. There will be brand related responsibilities, some live sessions with fans, interviews and other responsibilities. These are important so you can't run from them. A talent manager can help you here. He can be your best friend taking care of everything about the business.

There are many managers that are solely dedicated to managing the talents or stars of YouTube. Of course, you will have to pay him. The money he gets depends on how well you are doing and how much work he is doing.

Most popular and busy vloggers have talent managers who manage their business like any other manager in an office. They will do it all for you, such as assisting in brand deals, getting you better deals, negotiating for you, assisting fan related commitments, managing official meetings.

Before you hire a talent manager, study his track record. He will be representing you, so you need to get the best one out there. And, of course you should be in a position to afford him. There is no sense in hiring a talent manager who demands more that you earn from your channel. It is important to be smart and take a wise decision.

Before you decide that you need a talent manager, you need to be sure of your reasons for the same. If you are not serious about your business, then you will only waste your time and money on the MCN.

At a later stage, when you are extremely popular, you will surely need a talent manager to manager your work. But, till you reach that point, you need to think twice. Do you just need a talent manager because all popular vloggers have one? Can you afford him? Do you have some real problems that he can solve? You should question yourself before you just go out there looking for a talent manager.

You need to focus on providing content at a regular basis. Anything and everything will only be secondary. If you don't do this, then no matter what you do, it is not taking you anywhere. This is for sure.

## 2. How to find the right MCN?

Once you are sure that you need a talent agency to expand your reach, you will have to select the one talent manager you would want to go with. There are many talent management companies or talent agencies today. They can help with all that you need regarding your vlogging.

While there are some talent agencies that are general and cater to all kinds of vlogs, there are certain agencies that are dedicated to a specific format. For example, there are talent agencies that deal only with vloggers into fitness business.

Similarly, there are some that deal only with beauty and makeup. You need to find out the best ones in your domain. Start out by visiting the official websites of the talent agencies that you think will solve your purpose. The official website of the agency will give you all the relevant and important information that you need.

You should lay special emphasis on the clients of the agency. The official website will have a list of popular vloggers that they manage or have managed in the past. This is where you can assess how helpful they have been to other vloggers and how helpful they can be to you. Most websites will give you an idea of the pricing you can expect. If not, you can always enquire about this when you contact them personally.

You should also understand the criteria they have for accepting your application. A talent management agency will not put its efforts into anything that is not profitable. For example, a certain talent agency could have the criteria that you should have a certain number of followers. This makes them believe that you are serious about the work you do.

The process for application to the talent agency will also be mentioned in the website. You should make sure that you understand the entire process properly and clearly. You would be required to pitch in the idea as to what you can bring to the table. You should make sure that you can make them believe that they will only benefit with you in their line-up of clients. You should display enthusiasm and excitement to work with them.

There are many talent agencies that you can choose from. If you are looking for talent agencies in United Kingdom, the biggest names are Gleam Futures, OP Talent and Mode media.

**Gleam Futures**

Gleam Futures is a very popular talent management agency. In fact, it is the leading and the largest talent agency in the United Kingdom. In the year 2010, it was founded by Dominic Smales.

Dominic wanted this company to be a consulting firm for various brands that are keen on working on YouTube. It was a consulting firm that catered specifically to social media. But with time, the company has grown its interests and has widened its scope and work area.

Gleam Futures describes itself as a talent management agency now. It was Dominic who was responsible for spotting how profitable YouTube had become for both vloggers and agencies supporting them.

He understood that if his company associated itself with the rising stars of YouTube, it could only mean great revenue for both the parties. He knew that with time, this vlogging craze will only increase. So, it was but natural for him to tap into this market.

Dominic came across the vlog of Nicki Chapman and Sam. They had a very popular vlog called Pixiwoo. This vlog caught his imagination and he could not help but contact these vloggers. He knew that this was a growing market and he should not lose the opportunity to exploit this area. Nicki Chapman and Sam were his earliest clients and from there started his interest in managing vloggers and their business.

Every video that these two vloggers posted online brought them in the top rankers of YouTube. They were always amongst the highest viewed. After signing Pixiwoo, he worked to get them brand deals. He succeeded in getting them a make-up brand deal. It happened to be a great deal for the vloggers, brand and Gleam Futures. This was just the beginning. After that Dominic has worked with many great vloggers. He manages them and helps them to get brand deals among other things.

His elite client list includes Marcus Butler, Jack Maynard, Claire Marshall, Cat Meffan, Katie Snooks and Pointlessblog. They have offices both in UK and US. You can contact them very easily by sending them a query on their website or calling up their office numbers.

## OP Talent

Liam Chivers found OP Talent in the year 2012. He was ahead of his time. He knew that the vlogging business had a lot of unexploited areas. He quit his job to concentrate on this venture solely. OP Talent works with some great brands that offer up to six figure deals to the clients. These brands depend on OP Talent to grow and increase their reach. They wish to influence more and more number of people.

In the beginning of his career as a talent manager, Liam Chivers associated with KSI, who was popular but had only 100,000 subscribers at that time. Liam Chivers took a risk but helped KSI to grow up to 15 million today. This association has benefitted not only KSI, but also OP Talent. It is a leading agency for vloggers today.

This talent agency has a keen interest in video gaming. They are known to manage vloggers who have video gaming as their main theme. In fact, the 'OP' in the 'OP Talent stands' for over powered, which is a term used in the gaming world.

Endemol Shine, a leading media company, bought OP Talent in the year 2016. This only goes to prove the power and reach of OP Talent. If a media giant is interested in buying you, you have to have something special? It is time that media companies start to notice that vloggers and their channels are slowly taking over every other source of entertainment around.

The company has an influential list of vloggers. They share about forty million subscribers amongst them.

## Mode Media

Mode Media was found in the year 2004. It was called the Glam back then. The talent agency was created with the aim to help bloggers connect with various brands. Soon, Mode Media started helping all kinds of content creators. They started with only twelve clients, but as of now they have more than 6000 content creators under them. These content creators are both bloggers and vloggers.

They have a channel or website that has over 25 million followers. If you are chosen by this talent agency, they will not leave any stone unturned to promote you and your channel. Mode Media covers all kinds of themes in vlogging, be it make-up, fashion, health, food, education, parenting or clothing.

They are interested in all kind of vloggers. You can apply to them if you think they can do something great with your vlogging career. It should be noted that like many other talent agencies, they have a heavy screening process before they accept a vlogger. The acceptance depends on how popular the vlogger already is and if he is useful to Mode Media.

They come up with campaigns every now and then as they have great brands, such as Reebok and GNC working with them. It is important for the talent agency to make the right deal between the vlogger and the brand because it will ultimately affect their business as a media company.

The screening process ensures that the vlogger will be used for some lined up campaign or deal. They have clients like vloggers Steve Booker and Cassey Ho.

### 3. Collaboration with other vloggers

Another way to increase your current revenue and expand your reach as a influencer is collaboration with other artists. Imagine two of your favourite vloggers coming together to do a video, wouldn't you love that. Viewers always appreciate hard work and innovation. At the same time, they also want variety. If you had to eat the same food for the rest of your life, how would you feel? The viewers also look for variety.

Collaboration is a great opportunity for the viewer and for you. If you are able to create something entertaining while teaming up with another artist, you will also attract the subscribers of the other vlogger. If you know any vlogger with whom you can team up with, you should contact him.

If you have no direct contacts, then your talent manager can help you do this. He can help you get into the right deal. The talent manager understands your style and the other vlogger's style, so he will make sure that you both strike a golden deal. His reputation as a manager is at stake, so you can be sure that he'll do his best.

When you are preparing for collaboration, you should make sure that you maintain the style and persona that your audience love you for. You should make sure that the vlogger that you are deciding to collaborate with has a theme that adds to your work in some way.

It is also important that the vlogger has some following. Why would you collaborate with a vlogger who has 100 subscribers when you have around 2000? These are the issues that the talent manager will solve for you, but make sure that you understand these points well. You should sign the deal only when you are sure.

## 4. Talent Events

If you have been an avid follower of a renowned vlogger, you might have attended a live session with him. Even if you haven't, you might still know of the various events that are organised by YouTube for its star vloggers. Like the many other vloggers who get to be a part of these events, even you can get there someday.

YouTubers who have millions of subscribers are no less than celebrities. They are influencers as they have the means and strength to influence millions of fans. These events are organized in different parts of the world. These events offer a great chance for the vlogger to interact with his friends and maybe perform for them live. It is an opportunity to get on the stage and face the audience who already loves you.

The audience also have a great opportunity to see and meet the stars of YouTube. They can meet them and ask them questions. As a viewer, you will need to buy the tickets and passes. These events are slowly becoming very popular. Each year, things are better than the last year.

There are many vloggers that are totally breaking ground with their innovative and out of the box ideas. They are innovating new ways to earn money from something as simple as vlogging their daily life. Vlogger Joe Sugg (aka Thatcher Joe) is one such vlogger who keeps breaking his own records each time. He is a British vlogger who is popular for videos in which he never shies away from making fun of himself and his life. Could somebody make millions by making fun on himself? Well, Joe Sugg definitely can.

He plays pranks, tries hot yoga, and throws singing challenges on himself to keep the viewers hooked. He has over 8 million subscribers on YouTube, and the number is steadily increasing. He is very popular and owing to popularity, he takes parts in talent events and book signing events to generate revenue.

He was recently in news because of his 24 hour vlogging marathon. This marathon was one of its kind, and it managed to garner a lot of interest from his followers. He generated a lot of enthusiasm amongst people who watch him and comment on his videos by introducing a pair of micro pigs in the marathon.

This also helped him to attract more and more people to his channel. He was able to garner over a billion views for his 24 hour marathon live stream. Not only did he manage to increase his viewership, he also made the micro pigs very popular. People are searching more about them on Google. This is the power of vloggers. They can influence people in more ways than one. As a vlogger, you have the opportunity to re-invent and influence at the same time.

If you are a popular vlogger and have many followers with a number of views on your videos, you can be a part of some exclusive deals. For example, if you have a horse, a pig,a buffalo, a dove, a pigeon or a Labrador, these animals will also get as popular as you when you introduce them in your videos. These animals will have a lot of searches and other people can then do deals with you.

You can recommend or mention a product or put an affiliate link to that product on your website. You will be amazed at how positively people will take to this. This is a unique way to finalize various deals.

# Chapter 11: Finding sponsors

After you have made great content and done your end of marketing to increase your subscribers, the next obvious thing is to discover better ways to increase revenue.

If you study various successful vloggers, you will realize that a major part of money that they earn from vlogging is thorough sponsored content. As a vlogger, you can do the same. You will be required to advertise a particular brand on your YouTube channel.

Basically, you will create content for them and post the video on your channel. The brand can also use the same video on their channel. Such an arrangement is beneficial for both the vlogger and the brand. If the brand associates itself with the right vlogger, it can direct many followers of the vlogger to its own channel.

So, in a way the brand is becoming more popular. What else would a brand want? As a vlogger, you can earn money by hosting the brand's content. The amount you earn will depend on the kind of brand and also on your personal popularity.

You might have noticed the most popular beauty vloggers promoting brands on their channel. If the vlogger has many followers, it is a good deal for the company because it is reaching out to more people. If you are aiming at associating yourself with the top brands, then you should know that a highly rated brand will associate with you if you have something to offer to them.

When you are working on a deal with a brand or sponsor, the brand will try to negotiate the price. You will also be given a chance to present your case to the brand. It is said that if you are a popular vlogger with over a millon subscribers, you can earn around 10,000 pounds from one brand deal.

While you are all excited to sign brand deals, you should know that you have to be very careful about the deals that you sign. If your vlog channel has more advertisements than content, you will lose your viewers. While promoting brands is essential for a vlogger to generate revenue, you can't put that in the face of the viewer. Your viewers have associated with you because you give them something they want. If they realize that you are only interested in making money, you will lose your audience.

The brands that you are associated with will also not renew their deal with you in the future because they are with you because you are viewed. And, once you lose a substantial number of viewers, you also lose the brand. This is like a vicious cycle where only you are at the loser's end. The viewers have many vloggers on the Internet and the brands also have so many of them to hire.

The Advertising Standards Agency is the body that governs the brand and vlogger deals. There are a set of guidelines that you will have to follow when you sign a deal. After you sign a deal, you are obligated to follow the rules and regulations of the Advertising Standards Agency. So, it only makes sense to acquaint yourself well with all the rules that have been set regarding sponsored content.

According to the Advertising Standards Agency, the word 'advert' should be there in the thumbnail or title of the video. This is to inform the viewer that it is paid content. The description box should also have a mention that it is an advertisement. This is YouTube's way of keeping the viewers informed. The viewers can easily differentiate between a normal vlog video and the sponsored advertisement video.

As explained earlier, you should keep a check on the number of deals that you sign. If you get too greedy, your subscribers and the viewership will only decline. There is nothing worse than a viewer realizing that his favourite vlogger is more interested in money and will endorse any product for money.

The rule that you can keep for yourself is that you should work only for those brands that have something to do with your vlog. It is extremely important that the brand should fit well with the ideology of your brand. Your greed should not over power you here. In order to earn money, you shouldn't go about accepting each brand proposal that you get. There are many examples from which you can learn and adapt. There are many successful vloggers that get great deals almost every day from various brands, but they refuse because if you accept everything, your viewers will start rejecting you.

There are many vloggers who lost on viewership traffic when they started to advertise a lot for other brands. You have to earn money, so you need the support of a few good brands. But, you should know how to strike a balance. As a vlogger, everything that you do should be secondary to your viewers and your vlog.

## 1.How to find brands?

It is important to find the right brands for yourself. There are two ways to get brand deals. The two ways are as follows:

- You can contact the brands directly
- You can have an agent in the middle that helps you to get the best deals

### Various digital marketing agencies

A simple way to get the best deals for your vlog is to look for an agent, someone who acts as a middle man between you and the brands. These agents are called the digital marketing agencies and companies or the sponsorship platforms.

These digital marketing agencies are the ideal platform for a vlogger who doesn't want to get into the trouble of finding suitable brands.

There are many digital marketing agencies available that can help you get the best deals for yourself. The best one today is Famebit. Famebit is a very popular digital marketing agency that has helped many vloggers and brands connect with each other. It is quite simple to join this agency.

The requirement they have is that you should have at least 5000 subscribers on your channel. If you have reached this level then join Famebit today. If you haven't, then work on increasing your subscribers first.

Famebit and many other similar agencies work in a simple manner. You register with them if you have the desired number of subscribers that they want. As and when various brands that are registered with them post a sponsorship deal, you will get a notification.

You can apply if you like the deal. Based on your proposal, the brand will decide to go with you or not. You should not take this process very personally. There are many deals with various brands. Sooner or later, you'll crack one. So, be patient. Famebit, in particular will give you opportunities to get deals from 100 dollars to over 1000 dollars. Once you have signed the deal with the brand, 10 per cent of the sponsorship amount will go to Famebit.

When a brand opens a deal, you would be required to send in a proposal. You should make sure that you send in a proposal that the brand likes and finds interesting. It is not a great idea to have a common draft for all the brands that you will apply for.

It is more important to be specific. Study what the brand is looking for and send in the proposal accordingly. You need to prove to the brand that you are genuinely interested and that your proposal will only benefit them. Once the deal is signed, you will be given a time limit when you would be expected to submit the sponsored content. The content will be approved by the brand and it will go online.

**Contacting the brands directly**

While you can completely depend on digital marketing agencies to help you get sponsored content, you can also go a step further and contact the brands directly. This should be done especially when you have some knowledge about the brands that are doing well with vloggers of your kind.

If you think that your digital marketing agency is not helping you get in touch with the brands you like, then you can approach them directly.

Each brand has a PR department or a marketing department. This department is where all the brand related promotions are worked out. You would have to send a proposal to this department. Before you just draft a proposal and send it thorough, you need to be sure of what you are doing. You need to be as professional as possible. It is better to wait and prepare than hurrying your way and then making mistakes.

To begin with, you should make a list of all the brands that you are interested in working with. You should also understand that there are different kinds of brands, the local brand, the national brand and the international brand.

While it is easier to contact a local brand, it requires a little more professional approach to make contact with the national and international brands. Once you have made a list of all the brands that you wish to work with, divide the brands as per whether they are local, national or international. This will sort out your list and you have a better idea of what needs to be done with what brand.

The local brands are easier to approach. These brands will be in your areas. You can probably walk into the office of such a brand or take an appointment and visit. There is a chance that as you are looking for an opportunity to work with the brand, the brand could be looking for a vlogger like you to promote their business.

It is also important to study a brand carefully before you decide to send them a professional proposal. You should clearly understand what the brand stands for and what their vision is. This will help you to be to the point and precise when approaching the brand.

**2. A good proposal**

Once you have shortlisted the brands that you wish to work with, you need to contact them individually. An in-depth study of each brand is essential. It is very important that you send across a great proposal to the brand so that they take notice of your proposal. You have to understand that the brand could be getting hundreds of proposals like yours, so you need to stand out. Initially, you can only do this by writing a good proposal.

This section will help you to approach the brand of your choice in the most professional and efficient way. The following points will help you to understand what needs to be done:

**A personalised email:** When you are approaching a brand, you have to make a direct contact. If you think that you can send a general email saved in your drafts to every brand, then you will only be disappointed with all the rejections that you will face. When you have made an attempt to study about the brand, the next step is to contact them personally. An email will allow you to put your proposal forward and will also give the brand time to respond as per their schedule.

You should not send the proposal to an email ID that is not directed to a specific person. You will easily find the inquiry email ID of the brand online, but this is not the email ID you need. You need to contact the brand manager or at least someone from the marketing department. If the official website of the brand company does not provide you with this information, then you can put out a message on all your social media accounts. Maybe there is someone in your contacts who can help get a relevant email of the company. You can also use LinkedIn to find the right contact. There is a good chance that you will find the email from there.

The next step is to formulate a great email. Do not write an essay. The brand manager is a busy man and he might not be too interested in your lengthy proposal. Keep it short and professional. It is important to say all that you want in the least possible words. Make sure that you include the right information about you and your vlog. Also, propose how you can be an asset for the brand.

After the email is ready and you have the relevant email, you need to make sure that you put in the right subject line. There are many people who might think that this is not something very important. You might be surprised to know that the right subject is almost as important as choosing the best title for your vlog. It is the first thing that will catch the brand manager's attention. It needs to be catchy, yet professional if you want it to work in your favour.

While you are waiting for the brand to knock at your door with the best deal, you need to remember that there are many factors that a brand needs to consider. Even if the company rejects your proposal, you don't need to take it personally. There is a chance that the brand is not looking for sponsored content at the moment. There is also a chance that the company has exhausted the funds allocated to marketing and advertisements. So, don't get disheartened if you are turned down. You should keep looking and you'll find some great deals for yourself in the future.

**A media kit:** If the brand is interested in your proposal, they will email you for a media kit. This is a kit that you don't need immediately after you approach the brand. But, to save yourself from the last minute pressure and confusion, you should be ready with the media kit. This makes your work easier. You will just have to send the media kit across once a brand asks you for the same. It is very important that you take all the possible care while planning your media kit. This kit is like your business card. It will be used as your representation to assert what you and the channel stand for. Make sure that this representation is valid, concise and useful for you.

A media kit should essentially consist of the following things:

- To begin with, you should have a photograph of yours in the media kit. The brand is very much interested in knowing how you look because you are looking forward to being hired by them. You will be the face of the brand on the Internet, so it is only important that the brand makes sure that you look a certain way.

Don't assume that the brand has already seen you. Your vlog channel might be popular, but there is a chance that the company knows nothing about it. You need to make sure that you include a good photograph that is shot in a good light.

- You should provide your correct and up-to-date bio to the brand. The brand would want to know what you and your vlog stand for. You should provide the information about your vlog and the kind of videos you do.

You should also be able to explain how your vlog can support their brand. There should be enough evidence in the kind of videos you have done to prove that the brand will benefit if you associate with them.

- The brand might also be interested in knowing of any awards that you have won for your vlog. You should include them in your media kit. This will help the brand to understand how well your vlog has been doing. These awards could be a good recognition for you.

- The brand is interested in the numbers, more than anything else. They want to know exactly how many people you can influence. You should provide them with the number of subscribers that you have. The number of subscribers is an indication of your popularity. This will help the brand assess whether they will benefit from you in the long run or not.

- While you have mentioned the number of subscribers on your channel, the brand will be more interested in knowing the average views that your vlog gets. What if you have 10,000 subscribers, but only 1,000 of them are your regular viewers. It is necessary that all your subscribers will watch all your videos. You should calculate your average views and provide the information to the brand in your media kit. The average views can be calculated by calculating the average of the views you have managed to garner on your last five videos. This should be your parameter of success to the brand.

- The brand will be very interested in knowing some specific details of your popularity. They would be interested in your demographics and geographical popularity. In which countries and states are your videos most viewed? What age group do you most appeal to? If you don't fall in the age group and location that they wish to impress, then what is the point of working with you? So, make sure you inform the brand about these details in your media kit.

- You should also mention all the social media handles that you use. You should also mention the number of people that follow you on all these accounts.

If you are very popular and you have many followers on various social media platforms, why wouldn't the brand consider you? The brand needs to market its product through you, so they want someone who has many followers. This is how the message will be spread. It is very important for a vlogger to be very active on various social media platforms.

- You should also share some testimonials if you have any. These testimonials are like a proof of how influential your vlog is.

- The brand might also be interested in knowing of any media mentions that you have had in the past. You should include them in your media kit. This will help the brand to understand how popular you are as an influencer. A brand will only try to associate with you if they are sure that you can make an impact.

- If there is anything about the vlog that you feel makes you and the vlog special, you should go ahead and make it a part of the media kit. This might help you gain a deal with the brand.

- Your media kit should definitely contain your accurate contact details. What if the brand wants to contact you? Make it easier for the brand, and make sure that you include your contact details in the most precise way. Now, keep your fingers crossed because you have done your work. Just wait and hope for the brand to contact you.

**Telephone:** While you have sent the personalised email to the brand manager, you can still make a call to the brand office. After you have sent the email, give them some time to reply. If you think that the brand has not replied in a very long time, then you should call them. It is fine to ask about the status of your proposal.

There are times when people get too shy to make a phone call. You are not asking for any favours. You are just looking for the status of your application. You are a budding vlogger, the last thing you need to be is timid and shy.

The best approach is to wait for a certain amount of time and then make that call. Either they will say yes and ask you for the media kit or they will reply with a no. It is okay to ask for the reason of a no in case that is the answer, but don't be too pushy and harsh. You should remember that they have the right to reject you.

If the brand is polite enough to give you an answer for rejecting you, you should make sure that you work in that area. There are many brands out there, and you will definitely get more chances, but it is important to keep improving along the way. There is no point in committing the same mistakes again and again.

You should be patient while working through all this. There will also be some disappointments on the way. You need to be prepared for them. Make sure that you sound confident when you make that telephone call. Don't sound desperate and keep it as professional as possible. It is important to be positive and enthusiastic through this all. Your positivity and enthusiasm can actually impress the brand and can help you to get that deal.

## 3. What to do when the brand says yes

What if the brand likes your media kit and decides to give you a shot? What if the ball is in your court now and you get to decide? While you are ready to motivate yourself and get back on your feet if the brand says no, you also need to know what you should do if the brand is interested in working with you. It is important that you remember that you have to take the final decision. It is only important that you are all prepared.

You should stop being nervous and should ask the company that you want to meet. If they are interested in your work, they will agree. In case they are still contemplating, you will find them postponing the meeting. The job at your end is to try and fix a meeting.

Once the brand is ready to meet you, you should remember to put your best foot forward. You don't have to agree to all that they say and want. You need to know how you want to work. It is important that you understand this right from the very beginning. It is a business proposal and you have as much right to comment and demand as the brand.

Make sure that you are realistic when you are setting your expectations. You can't expect a brand to pay you millions and billions just like that. You should know where you stand as a vlogger. Understand your own strengths before making a move.

Plan in advance what you will wear for the meeting. Your first impression is as important as the popularity of your vlog. You should be dressed well and should appear cool and confident. No brand wants to sign an unsure and confused person. You should also work on the prices that you wish to charge. Research, think and fix what you would be asking for.

You should practice the entire meeting in your head and in your room. You should stand in front of the mirror and practice talking about the prices. The brand will most definitely try to negotiate and bring down your prices. You need to be prepared for this well in advance.

You should be quoting prices according to the work that you would do and the support that you would render. If you only do a mention for them in one of your videos or few of your videos, you will definitely quote a lesser price than if you do a complete and full video on them.

If you have a blog or website that is in associated with the vlog, you can also promote the brand there. These are the options that you will be providing the brand. It is always good to provide the brand with many options and let them choose the best one for them. This also shows your preparation and confidence.

You have to work on the prices according to your own popularity and need to work with the brand. For example, you can keep the price of a video on the brand for about 300 pounds. Any add-ons from there on should be priced higher. If they wish for a Facebook or Instagram mention, you could look at 200 pounds for each mention.

You can only make such a claim if you are able to prove that you will help the brand to increase its popularity. The number of subscribers that you have will help you in this case.

It is important that you know your ground reality. Successful vloggers are earning over 5000 pounds for a single sponsored content video. But, you can't demand the same. You need to be at that level. In the beginning, start slow.

You should work on the prices depending on the brand that you are contacting. If the brand is well known, you can look at better prices. The best policy is to work on preparing package deals for the brands. You could deliver a video and add-ons in a range of 500 to 1000 pounds. You could work on creating various such deals. A bigger brand will feel more responsible and committed towards you for a 1000 or 1200 pounds. A 500 pound deal could be too cheap for them. On the other hand, a smaller company can't afford a 1000 or 1200 pounds. Even a 500 pounds deal in marketing is huge for them.

Once the brand company has decided which the package deal that they want is, you need to seal the deal. Make sure you talk about the payment options clearly with the brand. It is better to talk about such things in the very beginning. After you have put up the sponsored content, you will be expected to send the invoice.

The brand should ideally pay you within 30 days, but there are some brands that could take longer. As the content provider, this is your right to ask them how much time they would require to process the payment. You should agree on something that you are comfortable with.

It goes without saying that you should also pay the tax of your business earnings. Register your business with the authorities and pay your tax. This is important because sometimes you might just forget that this needs to be done. This will only lead to problems for you in the future.

# Chapter 12: Case studies for inspiration

While you are working hard on various aspects of your vlog, a little inspiration will not hurt. In fact, it will only inspire you to give your best. When you hear of examples of some real people who started pretty much at your level and rose to great heights, it fills you with hope that even you can do so.

All the vloggers that have been mentioned in this section started out at a very basic level. Even they were always looking out for ways to better themselves. But with consistent efforts, they have reached a point where they have become an inspiration to many new and old vloggers.

A bit of research will tell you that there are all kinds of vloggers out there. You need to pick up something that works the best for you. There are the gaming vloggers who commentate on a game they are playing. Their principal ability is their capacity to think of fresh and novel methods for doing so.

The second most prevalent vloggers are the beauty vloggers. These vloggers guide on everything from makeup to clothes to latest trends in fashion. The third kind of vloggers are daily vloggers. These vloggers simply began discussing themselves and their lives to the camera in their rooms. This is a very popular style of vlogging.

There are also educational vloggers and travel vloggers. New trends inspire new breed of vloggers. You should be on the lookout for what is trending these days.

If you study these vloggers carefully and closely then you will realize that they mastered some of the essentials of this business. While one is a king of content, the other is unbeatable in editing.

It is important that you understand their journeys and use the learning to improve your vlogging. As a newbie, there is so much that you should be learning. It is only right that you start learning right now and that too from these extra-ordinary vloggers.

This chapter discusses some vloggers and their journeys to help you in your respective journeys. The following case studies are shared so that they help you in your journey of vlogging:

## 1. PewDiePie

PieDiePie, aka Felix Arvid Ulf Kjellberg, is one of the most popular vloggers today. You might have been a follower or at least you would have heard of his extra ordinary achievements. These particular vlogs are owned and operated by a Swedish vlogger by the name of Felix Kjelberg. Felix ventured into the vlogging world in the year 2010. This is the year when he started PewDiePie.

You might be surprised to know that it only took him two years to grow to one million subscribers. This is a feat in itself. How many vloggers can boast of doing so? You might think that he started at a point when there were not many vloggers in the business. This is true, but the real fact is that if there were less vloggers, there was lesser number of viewers. Those who started at that time are not enjoying the popularity that he is.

While he reached a million subscribers in about two years, he has over fifty million subscribers to this date. If you look at the number of views that he has achieved, then it is close to fifteen billion views on his vlogs. You don't need to get daunted by this number.

He didn't reach here in a day or even in a year. It took him years of hard work and consistency to reach to the point where is so successful. His channel mainly focuses on various games. He makes videos as a commentator to walk through these games and expresses his view points.

His followers admire him for his style of commentary and his invaluable knowledge that comes with practice and in-depth study about each game that he makes a video on.

Needless to say, he makes great revenue from his channel. In fact, his earnings are increasing exponentially each year. While he was able to earn around four million dollars three years backs, he earned about seven million dollars two years back. It is reported that last year, he managed to earn twelve million dollars.

## 2. KSI

Another popular vlogger who can be an inspiration for many is KSI. He is British by origin and is an actor, comedian and rapper. His channel is very popular amongst FIFA lovers because FIFA is the main theme of KSI. A point to be noted here is that he shares some insights about his daily life every now and then.

He also makes vlogs about other games. But, the FIFA is like his main agenda. He uses his acting skills to deliver some interesting commentary of the game. His followers definitely enjoy his unique style and personality.

KSI has over fifteen million subscribers and his popularity is only increasing with time. If you are looking at the figures that prove that he earns really well, then it is reported that he comfortably makes about two million dollars per year.

### 3. CaseyNeistat

The next vlogger that we will throw some light on is Casey Neistat. If you watch some of his videos, you will be impressed by his style and by his professionalism. His videos are brilliantly edited. If some vlogger needs a crash course on how to produce and edit a vlog well, then his vlogs are the thing to watch.

He is extremely professional and a look at his videos will tell you that he is very serious about what he does. He is not one of those vloggers who shoot some random stuff and throw it on the Internet. He shoots well and then edits it well. His hard work has been the key to his success.

Casey Neistat started his vlog channel in the year 2010. He was an instant success. It took him some time to get there. In fact, he earned his first million subscribers only after a few years of vlogging. But, then he became more and more popular and became four million subscribers strong. This popularity and the number of subscribers is only getting bigger. It is reported that he is able to earn over one million dollars per year from his vlogs.

If you wish to get as popular as him, it is important to learn from his discipline. You need to focus more as you get popular. It is important to enjoy your vlogging, but it is all the more important to be very serious about it. You should maintain the enthusiasm that you have today even years from now.

### 4. DanTDM

Another channel that you will find very interesting is DanTDM. Dan Middleton is a very popular vlogger who started in the year 2012. His main focus is also games. But, what is different about him is that he puts his focus on the games that are very popular with kids. He mainly makes vlogs about games that are played by children.

If you are wondering about what TDM stands for, then you should know that it is the acronym for the name 'The Diamond Minecraft'. When Dan

Middleton started his channel, his main focus was this particular game. He would make informative videos on it. Slowly, he moved to other popular children games.

Dan Middleton has over twelve million subscribers. He is one of the vloggers who are getting better with the passage of time. You should definitely learn from such vloggers. They can be a huge inspiration to you and help you to get better with your vlogging skills.

*Other well- known vloggers you can check out (in alphabetical order):*

Alfie, aka Alfred Sydney Deyes = King of vlogs, has +4.1 million subscribers

Bethany Mota, aka Bethany Noel Mota, has +8.8 million subscribers

Casper Lee, aka Caspar Richard Lee, has +4.5 million subscribers

ElrubiusOMG has +23.5 million subscribers

Eric Rap Battles has +20 million subscribers

Fernanfloo has +2.3 million subscribers

Jenna Marbles, aka Jenna N. Mourey, has +15 million subscribers

Jim Chapman, aka James Alfred Chapman, has +2.3 million subscribers

Louise Glitter has +1.9 million subscribers

Michelle Phan, has +7.8 million subscribers

NigaHiga has +19.3 million subscribers

Nigahiga, aka Ryan Higa, has +14.6 million subscribers

Shane Dawson, aka Shane Lee Vaw, has +6.6 million subscribers

Smosh, aka Ian Andrew Hecox, has +20 million subscribers

Tanya Burr, has +2.7 million subscribers

The Fine Bros, aka Benny and Rafi Fine, have +12.5 million subscribers

Tyler Oakley, has +7 million subscribers

Vegetta777 has +17.3 million subscribers

Vsauce, aka Micahel Stevens, has +8.9 million subscribers

Yuya has +17.8 million subscribers

Zoella, aka Zoe Elizabeth Sugg (already mentioned in this book) = Queen of vlogging

# Conclusion

Thank you again for buying this book!

I hope this book was able to help you in understanding the basics of vlogging and various ways to enhance your earnings from your vlog.

If you have decided to take the plunge into the vlogging world, then you should know that you have already taken the most difficult step. Once you decide that you want to be a vlogger and earn money from it, it only gets better for you. But, you just can't take a camera, shoot a video and upload in on the Internet. You need to learn the basics and master them well. Like any other business, it is important that you take the right steps at the right time. This book will help you to succeed.

There are many vloggers out there. Some of them are doing really well for themselves. But, they did not reach where they are just by a fluke. A lot of hard work has helped them to reach where they are. Well, if they could do it, so can you.

The ways and strategies discussed in the book are meant to help you to enjoy your vlogging journey by doing the right things. There are many people that get too excited in the very beginning and then just give up because they can't handle the pressure. You have to be prepared that this will be challenging, but you can handle it.

You should always make sure that you vlog about something that you are passionate about. This will take you ahead of many others who just vlog whatever is in trend. There are a few such simple things that you should know to take off as a vlogger. With practice and patience, you will reach great heights.

At this stage, you just need to take the right steps as a beginner. This book will help you to understand those tips and then finally adopt them in your vlogging style. It will only get better from here on.

Finally, if you found this book useful, please take the time to share your thoughts and post a review on Amazon or on which ever website you bought the book. It'd be greatly appreciated!

Thank you and good luck!

# References

http://smallbusiness.chron.com

http://www.vlognation.com

https://www.theguardian.com

https://moneypantry.com

https://www.quora.com

http://www.glamourmagazine.co.uk

https://vloggerpro.com

https://www.youtube.com

http://www.playsquare.co

http://www.moneymagpie.com

http://www.makemoneyinlife.com

http://www.bbc.co.uk

https://www.easyspace.com

http://www.digitalspy.com

http://fusion.kinja.com

http://www.wikihow.com

http://www.refinery29.com

https://www.ytravelblog.com

http://www.therichest.com

http://lifestyle.allwomenstalk.com

www.quora.com

https://www.thetoptens.com

https://www.careervillage.org

http://www.business2community.com

http://www.vlognation.com

http://whatis.techtarget.com